A Walker's Guide To
HARPERS FERRY
WEST VIRGINIA

A Walker's Guide To
HARPERS FERRY
WEST VIRGINIA

by Dave Gilbert

LIBRARY OF CONGRESS
CATALOG CARD NUMBER 82-63068

ISBN 0-933126-28-X

First Edition
First Printing March 1983
Second Printing March 1984
Third Printing June 1986

Second Edition
First Printing May 1988
Second Printing May 1990

Third Edition
First Printing July 1991

Maps and Diagrams by Dave Gilbert

Front Cover: Harpers Ferry from Maryland Heights.
Back Cover: Shenandoah Pulp Company mill ruins.
Unless otherwise noted, all photographs are by the author.

Additional copies of this guidebook are available from:
HARPERS FERRY HISTORICAL ASSOCIATION
P.O. Box 197
Harpers Ferry, West Virginia 25425

Table of Contents

HARPERS FERRY TODAY

THE WALKING TOURS

RESEARCH SOURCES

Acknowledgements

Maps in this guidebook have been compiled from United States Geological Survey topographic maps; from historical maps prepared by Charles W. Snell, David Hannah, Paul R. Lee II, and the Denver Service Center, all of the National Park Service; and from an 1849 survey map of Weverton drawn by William Dawson, Jr.

Several people made indispensable contributions to this book. I am particularly indebted to Hilda Staubs of Harpers Ferry National Historical Park for making the park's extensive reference library, research reports, and photo collection available to me. I'm also grateful to Dennis Frye and Todd Bolton for valuable information on Maryland Heights, Storer College, and other matters relating to Harpers Ferry National Historical Park.

For information on turbines and other machinery, I owe considerable thanks to William E. Worthington, Jr., of the Smithsonian Institution in Washington, D.C.; to Florence Brigham of the Fall River Historical Society in Fall River, Mass.; to Gary J. Arnold of The Ohio Historical Society in Columbus, Ohio; and to Albert V. James of the National Capital Region of the National Park Service in Washington, D.C.

For very helpful information on the Shenandoah Pulp Company, I'm grateful to Helen E. Arnold of the Potomac Edison Company in Hagerstown, Md., and to W.H. Henchey of Westvaco Corporation in New York City.

For valuable information on John H. Hall, I owe thanks to Ron Kley, Curator of the Maine State Museum in Augusta, Maine.

I am also indebted to the National Archives; the United States Patent Office; the Washington County Library in Hagerstown, Md.; the Handley Library in Winchester, Va.; and the Harpers Ferry Historical Association.

Index of Maps

Harpers Ferry Today

These old buildings on Shenandoah Street are typical of the many 19th century structures now protected in Harpers Ferry National Historical Park.

Introduction

Understanding Harpers Ferry

Much has been written about Harpers Ferry over the years. Thomas Jefferson, after visiting the place in 1783, described his vivid impressions of the natural setting.

"The passage of the Patowmac through the Blue Ridge," he wrote, "is perhaps one of the most stupendous scenes in Nature." And indeed, Jefferson was a well traveled man.

But other visitors have been less impressed. Two British travelers described "a most abominable village" here in 1835, pervaded by the "smell of coal smoke" and the "clanking of hammers" from the Armory workshops. New England journalist John T. Trowbridge, who visited Harpers Ferry after the Civil War, was also unimpressed:

"But while the region presents such features of beauty and grandeur," he wrote, "the town is the reverse of agreeable.... Freshets tear down the centre of the streets, and dreary hill-sides present only ragged growths of weeds. The town itself lies half in ruins."

These differing views are certainly not apparent in the sights and sounds of Harpers Ferry today. An air of quaintness greets the contemporary visitor. Neatly restored 19th century structures line clean, paved streets. Window trim is nicely painted, and brick and stone is pointed with fresh mortar. The ridges that surround Harpers Ferry and the confluence of the Potomac and Shenandoah rivers are alive with verdant forests. By all accounts, the town looks better now than it has at any time since Jefferson's visit over 200 years ago—a tribute to the restoration and preservation efforts of the National Park Service.

But this contemporary quaintness is terribly deceptive. The attractive building facades and awesome scenery mask many layers of eventful and tumultuous history. The numerous shops and buildings which today comprise the core of the Lower Town, for example, were but a small part of a booming industrial center that once boasted 3,000 residents. Along the banks of the Potomac and Shenandoah rivers, where sycamore and yellow poplar now flourish, stretched water-powered mills and factories with thousands of square feet of heavy industrial machinery.

John Brown's Raid presents another paradox between past and present here. One of the most popular visitor attractions at Harpers Ferry is the Armory's old fire enginehouse and watchman's office where John Brown was captured. But this simple, well-kept brick building has been dismantled and moved so many times that its outward appearance has changed considerably. It now sits several feet from its original location,

John Brown's Fort as it appears today in the Lower Town of Harpers Ferry.

which is covered by a tall railroad embankment. Gone are the surrounding Armory workshops and stores of muskets that John Brown came to seize. Gone also are the taverns and drinking houses that catered to the excited and angry locals who gathered when word of the raid spread. Ultimately, what is missing most is the immediacy of the event—the terrorized townspeople who still remembered the bloody 1831 Nat Turner slave rebellion in tidewater Virginia; the anxious militiamen who gathered from as far away as Martinsburg and Winchester; the grim, fanatical John Brown and his hapless hostages; and the brave U.S. Marines who finally stormed John Brown's "Fort" and ended the ordeal.

The natural setting has also changed since the first days of the white man's arrival. Timber on Loudoun Heights was assailed with ax, maul, and wedge to fuel iron furnaces and blacksmith forges, until by the Civil War only bare ground remained. On Maryland Heights, Union fortifications erected during the Civil War were replete with breastworks, artillery emplacements, and stone fortifications, but hardly a single living tree. The rivers were dammed with rock and rubble to harness precious water power, and cliffs were blasted away for building stone and to make way for road, railway, and canal.

Fortunately, nature has endured. The ridges that surround Harpers Ferry are once again alive with second growth hardwood forest. The scenic cliffs of Maryland Heights and Loudoun Heights still stand tall.

Bridge pier ruin on the Shenandoah River.

And to the delight of whitewater enthusiasts, the Potomac and Shenandoah rivers again run free.

This walker's guide is intended to help you explore the natural beauty and physical remains of Harpers Ferry, and to introduce a few of the more prominent people who rose or fell with the town's changing fortunes. This guide also attempts to penetrate the calm, peaceful setting evident today and to uncover, layer by layer, the town's fascinating, tumultuous history. Footpaths lead to crumbling stone foundations, second growth hardwood forest, abandoned sluiceways, weed-covered earthworks, and a small fire enginehouse that John Brown immortalized in 1859. Upon close inspection, there are compelling signs of the struggle here between man and nature, and between men themselves. The contrasts between past and present are real, but you must look for them.

Historical Chronology

1733—Peter Stephens settles at "The Hole" where the Potomac and Shenandoah rivers meet.

1748—Robert Harper purchases "The Hole" and operates the Potomac ferry.

1763—The town of "Shenandoah Falls at Mr. Harper's Ferry" is established by the Virginia General Assembly.

1786—George Washington tours Harpers Ferry as a representative of the Patowmack Company.

1796—The U.S. Government purchases 118 acres for a federal armory and arsenal at Harpers Ferry.

1820—John H. Hall comes to Harpers Ferry to manufacture his patented breech-loading rifle for the U.S. Government.

1832—The C&O Canal is completed to Lock 33 across from Harpers Ferry.

1833—The B&O Railroad reaches the Maryland shore opposite Harpers Ferry.

1859—Abolitionist John Brown raids the U.S. Armory and Arsenal at Harpers Ferry.

1861—Virginia secedes from the Union; the Harpers Ferry Arsenal is burned by retreating Federal troops.
1862—Stonewall Jackson surrounds and captures over 12,500 Union troops at Harpers Ferry.
1863—West Virginia separates from Virginia, becoming the 35th State.
1864—Philip Sheridan ransacks the Shenandoah Valley from his Union base at Harpers Ferry.
1870—The Flood of 1870 takes 42 lives and destroys the town of Virginius.
1884—Thomas Savery purchases the old Armory Grounds and Rifle Factory site at a U.S. Government auction.
1889—The Flood of 1889 ruins the last water-powered mill on Virginius Island.
1891—John Brown's Fort is sold and removed from Harpers Ferry.
1924—The Flood of 1924 closes the C&O Canal for good.
1935—The Shenandoah Pulp Company, Harpers Ferry's last water-powered factory, closes.
1936—The record Flood of 1936 crests at $36^{1}/_{2}$ feet in Harpers Ferry.
1944—A Congressional Act provides for the establishment of Harpers Ferry National Monument.
1968—John Brown's Fort is moved back to the Lower Town after a 72-year absence.

Ruins of old water inlet arches on Virginius Island.

The Walker's Guide

Harpers Ferry and the ridges that surround it are criss-crossed by a variety of trails in various states of repair and disrepair. The white-blazed Appalachian Trail, one of America's best known wilderness footpaths, passes right through the Lower Town of Harpers Ferry (see **Harpers Ferry Today** map, pages 14-15). This trail, which today extends over 2,000 miles from Georgia to Maine, is regularly maintained by member clubs of the Appalachian Trail Conference (ATC). The Potomac Appalachian Trail Club (PATC) is responsible for the Harpers Ferry section of the trail.

The Chesapeake & Ohio Canal towpath travels along the north bank of the Potomac River between Washington, D.C., and Cumberland, Maryland. This level, eight-foot-wide packed dirt trail is ideal for hiking, suitable for biking, and is regularly maintained by the National Park Service.

At the other end of the spectrum are old wagon roads, logging trails, and military roads dating from the 19th century. Some of these old trails have been incorporated into the Appalachian Trail and other well-marked public footpaths. But many more have been abandoned and reduced to mere deer tracks. These old paths are often impossible to find through the weeds and underbrush of late spring and summer. But during the winter months and early spring, these trails are much easier to follow and sometimes lead to secluded ruins or forgotten Civil War fortifications.

In between these extremes are the trails that criss-cross Virginius Island, the Grant Conway Memorial Trail on Maryland Heights, and the blue-blazed trails that branch off the Appalachian Trail. These trails receive various degrees of use, and are subject to various degrees of maintenance.

This walker's guide, in its effort to explore all aspects of the area's physical and natural history, includes trails from the entire spectrum described above. Whether you choose to stick to the flagstone sidewalks of Harpers Ferry or explore the most remote corner of Maryland Heights, you will find appropriate trails marked on the maps that follow.

Finding The Trails

To locate the starting point of a particular walking tour, refer first to the **Harpers Ferry Today** map on pages 14-15. Each of the guidebook's eight walking tours is numbered and its location is identified on this map. The roads that lead to the starting point are identified, and the location of parking is indicated.

Once you have identified the location of a particular walking tour, turn to the section of the guidebook that describes that specific tour (see **Table of Contents** for page numbers). The detailed maps for each separate walking tour show where the trails begin and where parking is located in relation to the trails.

After you have parked and locked your car, you're ready to go.

Reading The Trail Maps

Each trail map for each walking tour shows the primary trail route, secondary intersecting trails, and numbered points of interest. If a particular trail is marked by painted blazes, the color of the blazes is indicated on the trail map. For example, the white-blazed Appalachian Trail is marked "white". In most cases, all trails in a particular area, whether maintained or not, are shown on the trail map.

The numbered points of interest on each map are keyed to the accompanying text. Where appropriate or helpful, a written trail description accompanies this text in *italic* type. Such trail information might include:

- Approximate amount of time you should allow for a complete walking tour;
- Exactly where a trail begins, continues or ends;
- The general condition of a particular trail;
- The type of trail markings, if any, you will find;
- The physical topography along the way—a steep climb or a sharp descent, for instance.

Please be mindful that the trail information contained in this guidebook was as current as possible when we went to press. Changes in a trail route or in the condition of a trail periodically result from human decisions or natural occurrences.

For up-to-date trail information, stop in at the National Park Service Visitor Center on Cavalier Heights or at the Appalachian Trail Conference headquarters on Washington Street in Harpers Ferry.

Visitor Services At Harpers Ferry

Public Parking. The symbol **P** indicates the location of parking on the maps in this guidebook.

The main parking lot for Harpers Ferry National Historical Park is located on Cavalier Heights, about one mile west of the Shenandoah River bridge just off U.S. Route 340. Park Service shuttle buses transport visitors from here to the Lower Town.

(continued on page 16)

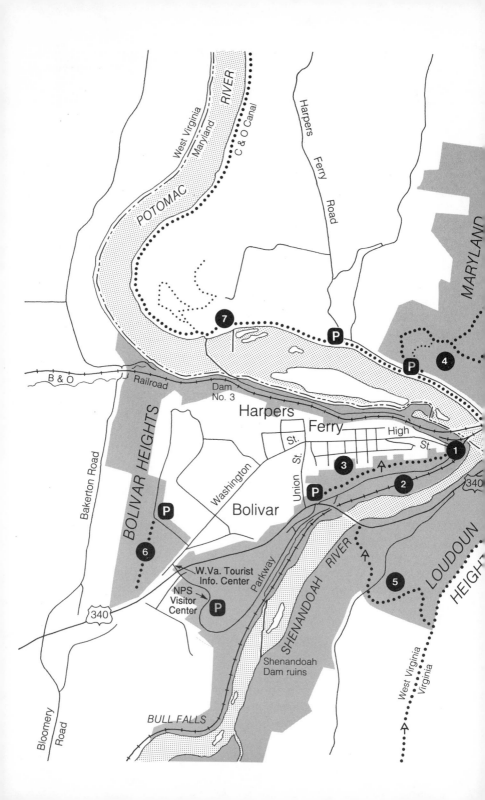

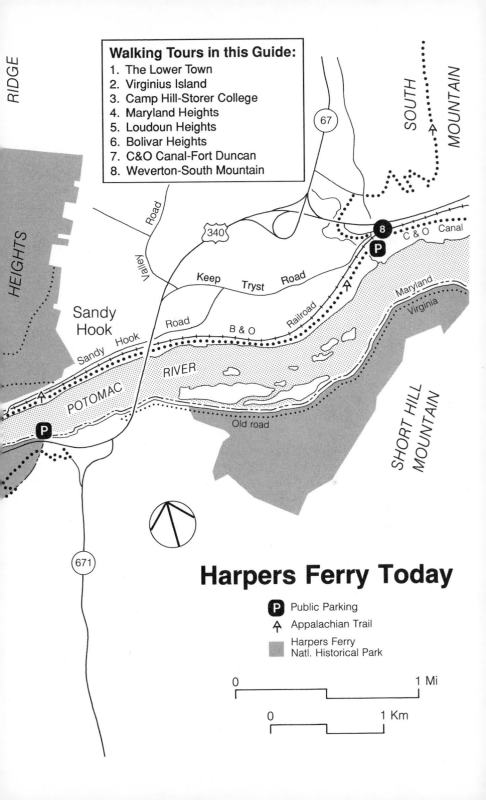

Walking Tours in this Guide:

1. The Lower Town
2. Virginius Island
3. Camp Hill-Storer College
4. Maryland Heights
5. Loudoun Heights
6. Bolivar Heights
7. C&O Canal-Fort Duncan
8. Weverton-South Mountain

RIDGE

SOUTH MOUNTAIN

HEIGHTS

67

340

C & O Canal

8

Valley Road

Keep Tryst Road

Sandy Hook

Sandy Hook Road

B & O Railroad

Maryland

Virginia

POTOMAC RIVER

Old road

SHORT HILL MOUNTAIN

671

Harpers Ferry Today

P Public Parking

⚐ Appalachian Trail

Harpers Ferry
Natl. Historical Park

0   1 Mi

0   1 Km

Smaller parking areas, with capacities ranging from four cars to over a dozen, are located at most trailheads for the walking tours in this guidebook.

National Park Service Visitor Center. The Visitor Center is located on Cavalier Heights adjacent to the park's main parking lot. Here visitors can obtain the schedules and locations of daily interpretive programs conducted in the Lower Town and other park locations, and obtain up-to-date information on trails in the area. A National Park Service Information Center is also located at the Stagecoach Inn in the Lower Town.

Interpretive exhibits that deal with the Armory, John Brown, the Civil War, Black History, and other topics relating to Harpers Ferry are located in various buildings throughout the Lower Town.

Rest Rooms. Public rest rooms are located on Cavalier Heights at the National Park Service Visitor Center and in the Lower Town next door to the Stagecoach Inn on Shenandoah Street.

Appalachian Trail Conference Headquarters. The ATC building is located on Washington Street in Harpers Ferry, about a half-mile from the Lower Town. Here visitors can obtain information on the Appalachian Trail and on other hiking trails in the Harpers Ferry area.

West Virginia Tourist Information Center. Travelers seeking West Virginia highway maps as well as local and state tourist information can stop at the West Virginia Tourist Information Center near Bolivar Heights, just across U.S. Route 340 from the National Park Service Visitor Center.

Shops and Restaurants. The towns of Harpers Ferry and Bolivar feature a variety of shops and restaurants. A list of these establishments is published by the Harpers Ferry-Bolivar Merchants Association, and is available at the West Virginia Tourist Information Center or at participating shops and restaurants.

Whitewater Rafting and Canoeing. The Potomac and Shenandoah rivers at Harpers Ferry offer challenging Class I, II, and III whitewater rapids and spectacular, unspoiled scenery. At the present time, three professional outfitting companies in the immediate area offer whitewater raft trips and canoe rentals. Stop at the West Virginia Tourist Information Center for more information and for a copy of each company's brochure.

1896 photograph of the Lower Town taken from Maryland Heights. The new B&O Railroad station in the foreground had just opened. (National Park Service photo).

The Lower Town

Allow about two and a half hours for this complete walking tour. Shenandoah and Potomac Streets are level, while High Street begins a fairly steep climb out of the Lower Town. St. Peter's Church and Jefferson Rock are reached after a steep climb up the Stone Steps and a paved footpath.

1. Shenandoah Street. In 1830, the Harpers Ferry, Charles Town & Smithfield Turnpike Company was organized. The following year the company's turnpike was completed to Harpers Ferry, becoming Shenandoah Street in the Lower Town. A toll was charged for travel on the turnpike, the rate being about two cents a mile for horse and buggy. In 1833, Shenandoah Street was macadamized—finished with small broken stones compacted into a solid layer. Today this surface has been re-created here.

2. Bridge Street. In 1843-1844, the Shenandoah Bridge Company erected a covered wagon bridge across the Shenandoah River. The bridge replaced the old "Shenandoah Rope Ferry" which had been operated by the U.S. Government since 1818. Crossing the river at the foot of Bridge Street, the structure was supported by two stone piers each 28 feet high,

17

30 feet wide, and ten feet thick at their base. The bridge had a double wagon track, was completely weatherboarded, and was roofed with cypress shingles.

Despite the completion of this new bridge, the U.S. Government still owned the ferry rights across the Shenandoah River. In return for not exercising these rights, the Shenandoah Bridge Company granted the government toll-free passage for all Armory workers and property using the bridge.

The bridge was demolished by a violent wind storm in June 1859, was rebuilt later that year, and was destroyed for good by Confederate raiders in June 1861. Not until 1882 was a new bridge erected across the Shenandoah River, this time about 300 yards downstream at The Point.

3. Winchester & Potomac Railroad. In March 1836, the Winchester & Potomac Railroad was opened 32 miles from Harpers Ferry to Winchester, Virginia. During the Civil War, between 1864-1865, the line served as a major troop and supply carrier for Philip H. Sheridan's Army of the Shenandoah. Today the line is part of the CSX system and is still in use.

4. Market House. The Market House was built on Armory property by the U.S. Government in 1846-1847. The two-story brick building was 60 feet long, 30 feet wide, and had large arched doorways on the first floor (see photo on page 41). From 1847 to 1868, this first floor served as the

A Union supply train passes a troop train at Harpers Ferry during the winter of 1864-1865. The locomotive has just crossed Bridge Street. (National Park Service photo).

18

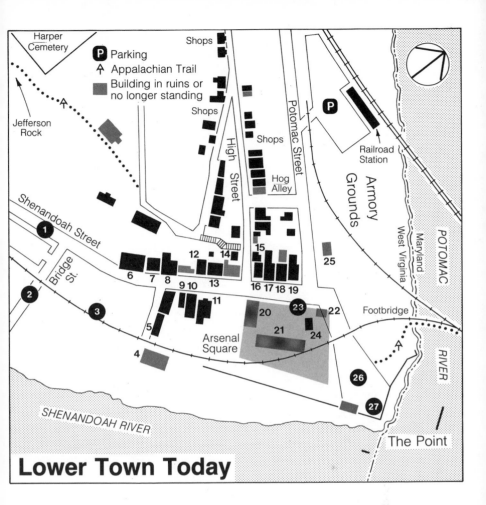

Lower Town Today

town market, where on Wednesdays and Saturdays vegetables, meat, poultry, cheese, eggs, and fish were offered for sale. The second floor was used as a meeting hall by the Sons of Temperance. The building was destroyed by the record Flood of 1936.

5. Flood Story. As settlers in the valleys of the Potomac and Shenandoah rivers cleared land for agriculture and cut timber to fuel iron furnaces and blacksmith forges in the 1800s, flooding became more frequent. Here at Harpers Ferry, where the waters of the Potomac and Shenandoah converge, periodic floods inundated the Lower Town and doomed homes and industry erected along the rivers. See **Memorable Floods At Harpers Ferry** on the next page.

(Walking Tour continues on page 22)

Memorable Floods At Harpers Ferry

1748. According to local legend, floodwaters drove Robert Harper from his log cabin at the corner of Shenandoah and Potomac Streets.

1753. "The Pumpkin Flood," so named for the great numbers of pumpkins washed down from the gardens of nearby Indian villages.

1852. The greatest flood since the first settlers arrived at Harpers Ferry. A four-story brick cotton mill on Virginius Island was leveled by the rampaging Shenandoah.

1870. The Shenandoah River rose so rapidly that residents were trapped on Virginius Island. Floodwaters claimed 42 lives and swept away almost all the island's homes and industry.

1877. High water caused considerable damage to the C&O Canal and closed the old Shenandoah Canal for good.

1889. The rivers rose to a record height—34.8 feet—carrying away the Shenandoah wagon bridge and leaving behind "filthy deposits" in the Lower Town.

Shenandoah Street after the 1889 Flood. (National Park Service photo).

1924. Floodwaters swept away three spans from the Bollman highway bridge across the Potomac River and permanently closed the C&O Canal.

1936. 36 1/2 feet—the all-time record crest at Harpers Ferry. The repaired Bollman Bridge and rebuilt Shenandoah bridge were swept away for good, while many businesses in the Lower Town were left in ruins.

Shenandoah Street during the 1936 Flood. (National Park Service photo).

1942. All-time record crest for the Shenandoah Valley—32.4 feet at Millville, West Virginia. Floodwaters reached 34 feet in the Lower Town.

1972. Floodwaters from Hurricane Agnes swelled to 29.7 feet here but caused relatively little damage.

1985. The Potomac and Shenandoah rivers crested at nearly 34 feet in Harpers Ferry, causing approximately $250,000 in damage. Paw Paw, West Virginia, and communities along the Potomac's South Branch were devastated by this flood.

Harpers Ferry at the height of the 1985 Flood.

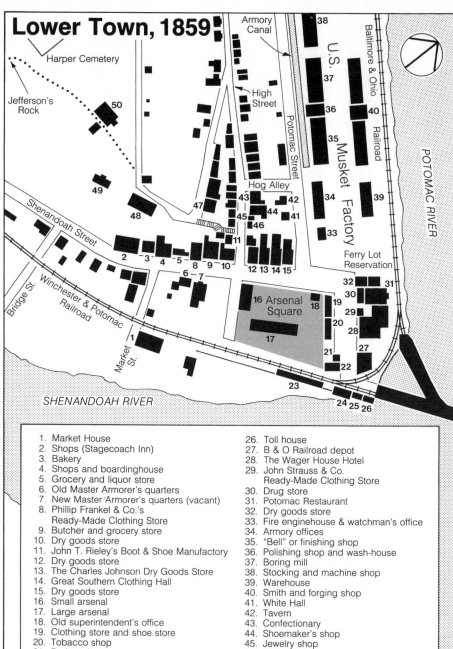

Lower Town, 1859

- Harper Cemetery
- Jefferson's Rock
- Armory Canal
- High Street
- Potomac Street
- Hog Alley
- Shenandoah Street
- Winchester & Potomac Railroad
- Bridge St.
- Market St.
- U.S. Musket Factory
- Baltimore & Ohio Railroad
- POTOMAC RIVER
- Ferry Lot Reservation
- Arsenal Square
- SHENANDOAH RIVER

1. Market House
2. Shops (Stagecoach Inn)
3. Bakery
4. Shops and boardinghouse
5. Grocery and liquor store
6. Old Master Armorer's quarters
7. New Master Armorer's quarters (vacant)
8. Phillip Frankel & Co.'s Ready-Made Clothing Store
9. Butcher and grocery store
10. Dry goods store
11. John T. Rieley's Boot & Shoe Manufactory
12. Dry goods store
13. The Charles Johnson Dry Goods Store
14. Great Southern Clothing Hall
15. Dry goods store
16. Small arsenal
17. Large arsenal
18. Old superintendent's office
19. Clothing store and shoe store
20. Tobacco shop
21. Barber shop
22. Jewelry store
23. Winchester & Potomac Railroad depot
24. The Gault House Saloon
25. B & O Railroad office
26. Toll house
27. B & O Railroad depot
28. The Wager House Hotel
29. John Strauss & Co. Ready-Made Clothing Store
30. Drug store
31. Potomac Restaurant
32. Dry goods store
33. Fire enginehouse & watchman's office
34. Armory offices
35. "Bell" or finishing shop
36. Polishing shop and wash-house
37. Boring mill
38. Stocking and machine shop
39. Warehouse
40. Smith and forging shop
41. White Hall
42. Tavern
43. Confectionary
44. Shoemaker's shop
45. Jewelry shop
46. Shop
47. Harper House
48. St. Peter's Roman Catholic Church
49. Catholic school
50. St. John's Protestant Episcopal Church

6. Stage Coach Inn. This 2 1/2-story building was erected in 1825-1826, and was originally used as a store and private residence. From 1830-1837, the building served as a hotel and was called the "Stage Coach Inn." An advertisement which appeared in the *Virginia Free Press* on April 7, 1830, described this hotel as "commodious and comfortable, and the rooms neat and pleasant." During this same year stage coaches operated between Washington, D.C., and Harpers Ferry on Tuesdays and Saturdays. Fare was four dollars and the trip was made in a day. Through the Civil War the old inn was used by the Federal Government as quarters for troops and as a military warehouse. The building now houses the National Park Service Bookshop and an Information Center.

7. Philip Coons Building. This three-story stone building was built in 1845-1846. A partition wall divided the first floor into two separate shops. At the time of John Brown's Raid, one of these shops was vacant and for rent while the other shop was occupied by the bakery of John Stonebraker. Exterior steps on the left side of the building led to a private residence on the second floor and to a Masonic meeting hall on the third floor. Public rest rooms are now located on the first floor.

8. McCabe-Marmion Building. Construction on this three-story building was completed in 1845. Two separate stores occupied the first floor at the time of the John Brown Raid: the grocery and liquor store of J.&J. Mathews and either a tailor shop or a shoemaker's shop. The upper floors were used as a boardinghouse. The Park Service has established a unique exhibit here on "How To Read An Old Building."

9 & 10. Old Master Armorer's Quarters. Building 10 was erected in 1812 as a drug store and private residence. In 1818, the U.S. Government acquired the house and used it as quarters for the Master Armorer until 1858. After the John Brown Raid in 1859, an Army Recruiting Office was opened in this building by a company of United States regulars sent to guard the Armory. Building 10 has been substantially enlarged since the Civil War and now houses a Dry Goods Store exhibit. Building 9 was erected after the Civil War.

11. New Master Armorer's Quarters. This brick house was built in 1858-1859 as quarters for the Master Armorer. John E.P. Daingerfield, the Paymaster's Clerk, occupied the house in 1859, and was one of several hostages taken by John Brown during his ill-fated raid. The building now houses an exhibit on the guns and gun-making machinery of the old Harpers Ferry Armory. See **Arms Manufacture In The 19th Century** on the next page.

12. William Richards Building. Erected in 1824, this building was occupied by "Philip Frankel & Co.'s Ready-Made Clothing Store" at the time of John Brown's Raid. Prior to the rise of manufacturer clothing, "respectable" men bought clothing custom-made from a tailor. But as the middle class grew during the 19th century, garments were mass-produced in a wide range of sizes, prices, and quality, making it harder to distinguish social classes by outward appearance. By 1860, there were four businesses in Harpers Ferry that specialized in "ready-made" clothing.

Arms Manufacture In The 19th Century

In the early 1800s, musket manufacture at the Harpers Ferry Armory was divided into four categories: lock, mounting, stock, and barrel.

The lock, or firing mechanism, was the most fragile and complicated part of the musket. The several lock components were carefully machined with forging, drilling, and filing tools. The mounting, which was comprised of trigger guards, bands, and heel plates, was machined very much like the parts of the lock.

The shaping of the gun stock was basically a hand operation in the early 1800s, requiring a single craftsman to whittle, bore, and chisel each stock. But in 1818, Thomas Blanchard introduced a lathe for turning irregular forms. The following year this machine was installed at the Harpers Ferry Armory. Blanchard's lathe, which in subsequent years was developed into 16 separate units, used a standard stock as a template from which to cut identical copies.

Producing the gun barrel was the most expensive and physically demanding part of arms manufacture. First a piece of bar iron was rolled into a long, narrow *skelp*. At the barrel forging shop this *skelp* was welded into a barrel. By 1840, waterpowered triphammers replaced manual methods of welding barrels at the Harpers Ferry Armory, producing a sounder seam in about half the time previously required. Annealing restored malleability to the gun barrel, rendered brittle by several heatings during welding.

Next the barrel was straightened by hand and the bore was drilled. In the proof house the barrel was charged with powder and ball to test the strength of the weld. A barrel that with-stood two charges was given a proof mark and sent back to the boring mill to be finish bored and polished. Finally, the barrel went to the finishing shop for final assembly with the lock, mounting, and stock.

On April 19, 1858, Philip Frankel & Co. placed the following advertisement in the *Virginia Free Press:*

New and Fashionable Spring and Summer
Ready Made Clothing

In addition to their large and well-assorted stock of
Ready-Made Clothing, they offer also a large stock of
Hats, Caps, Boots, Shoes, and Gentlemen's Furnishing Goods
Such as fine white Linen and Fancy Marseilles Shirts,
Under Shirts and Drawers, Overalls, Neck and Pocket
Handkerchiefs, Hosiery, Suspenders, Gloves, with a great
variety of Fancy Goods, such as Pocket Books, Combs,
Brushes, &c.

The building now houses a replica of Frankel's ready-made clothing store.

13. Tearney Building. The Tearney Building was erected in 1844, and was divided by partition walls into two sections. In 1859, a butcher and grocery store occupied one of the first floor shops. Typical grocery store items of this period included rice, cheese, prime bacon, sugar, molasses, Porto Rico, Rio, and Java coffee, Imperial, Uong Hyson, and Souchong tea, indigo, ginger, salt, fish oil candles, and a variety of other meats, fish, and spices.

14. John T. Rieley Building. This building was erected by John Wager, Jr., between 1804-1813, making it one of the oldest structures in the Lower Town today. On January 20, 1853, "John T. Rieley's Boot & Shoe Manufactory," which occupied the building, advertised in the *Virginia Free Press* that "they will manufacture in the very best manner, and out of the best material, all kinds of BOOTS AND SHOES. All work will be warranted to be of the best quality and workmanship. REPAIRING will also be neatly and substantially done, and on the shortest notice."

15 & 16. Ann C. Stephenson Building. From 1803-1838, the "Harpers Ferry Hotel," a spacious frame building with 22 rooms, stood along Shenandoah Street between High Street and Potomac Street. In 1838-1839, a large part of this old hotel was torn down and Building 15 was erected jointly with Building 17. Building 16 was added between 1840-1845. At the time of John Brown's Raid, Mrs. Ann C. Stephenson, an 82-year-old widow, lived in this addition. Building 16 now houses an exhibit on Storer College.

On the morning of October 17, 1859, Thomas Boerly, a town resident, was shot and killed by one of John Brown's raiders in front of the Ann C. Stephenson Building at the corner of High and Shenandoah Streets.

17. William Anderson Building. The William Anderson Building was erected jointly with the Ann C. Stephenson Building in 1838-1839. The first floor was occupied by "The Charles Johnson Dry Goods Store" at the time of John Brown's Raid.

18. John C. Unseld Building. For several years after 1838, a frame section of the old "Harpers Ferry Hotel" that had not been torn down was used here as a store and dwelling. The present brick building was erected in 1846-1847. Prior to the Civil War the first floor was occupied by the "Great Southern Clothing Hall" while the upper floors served as a boarding-house. The building now houses a John Brown exhibit.

19. Gerard Bond Wager Building. The log cabin of the town's first settler, Peter Stephens, stood on this site. In 1747, this cabin was occupied by Robert Harper. The present brick building was built in 1837-1838, and was first used as a tavern and eating house. A rear annex was added four years later.

20. Small Arsenal. Arms produced at the Harpers Ferry Armory were stored in two brick buildings here on a tract of land known as Arsenal

The Large Arsenal dominates this 1803 print of Harpers Ferry. The Potomac Ferry is pictured crossing the river. (National Park Service photo).

Square. By 1859, the entire lot was surrounded by a stone wall and high iron fence.

The Small Arsenal, a two-story brick building measuring 36 feet by 68 feet, was erected in 1806-1807. On April 18, 1861, the day after Virginia seceded from the Union, Lt. Roger Jones of the U.S. Army set fire to this building, preventing some 15,000 muskets and rifles from falling into Confederate hands.

21. Large Arsenal. Built in 1799-1800, this two-story structure measured 125 feet by 32 feet. By 1859, the building had fallen into such disrepair that only miscellaneous supplies and a detachment of U.S. regular Army troops sent to guard the Armory after John Brown's Raid were housed here.

The Outbreak Of Civil War

In the fall of 1860, Abraham Lincoln was elected our nation's 16th president. Southern states, outraged by the prospect of a Republican chief executive, leaned toward secession and on December 20, South Carolina withdrew from the Union.

In January 1861, Armory Superintendent Alfred M. Barbour, concerned by anti-Union sentiment in the Shenandoah Valley, advised the War Department that he had "reason to apprehend that some assault will be made upon the United States Armory at Harper's Ferry." In fact, a company of United States regulars had been stationed at Harpers Ferry to protect Armory property since John Brown's Raid.

In the spring of 1861 came the bombardment of Fort Sumter and Lincoln's call for 75,000 volunteers to put down the rebellion. On April 17, a Virginia convention which had been indecisive during the preceding months passed an ordinance of secession. The United States Armory and Arsenal at Harpers Ferry became an immediate military objective.

Lt. Roger Jones of the U.S. Army defended the Armory on the evening of April 18 with 50 regulars and 15 volunteers. In nearby Charles Town several companies of Virginia militia—360 men in all—assembled and advanced toward Harpers Ferry. Jones, outnumbered and unable to obtain reinforcements, set torches to the Armory and Arsenal buildings. At about 10 p.m. an explosion ripped through the Small Arsenal. Townspeople acted quickly to extinguish fires in most of the Armory buildings, but by the time the first Virginia militiamen entered town the Small Arsenal and some 15,000 arms were consumed by fire.

22. Superintendent's Office. In 1832, a one-story dwelling house here was converted into an office for the Armory Superintendent. In 1859, the building was used by the town of Harpers Ferry under a lease from the government as a Town Hall.

John Brown's Raid

On Sunday evening, October 16, 1859, 19 men of the "Provisional Army of the United States" gathered at the Maryland end of the covered railroad and wagon bridge at Harpers Ferry. This small force was led by John Brown, a 59-year-old abolitionist whose Pottawatomie Creek murders of pro-slavery Kansans had brought him to the nation's eye. The raiders, armed with Sharps rifles, captured the bridge watchman, entered Harpers Ferry, and seized the Armory grounds.

Brown had come to arm an uprising of slaves. But the few slaves the raiders could gather were possessed more by fright and confusion than fighting mettle. Instead an alarm was sounded. At midnight a shot from a raider's gun narrowly missed the bridge watchman's relief man. At 1:30 a.m. the eastbound express train from Wheeling was detained. In the commotion that followed, Heyward Shepherd, the station baggage man and a black freedman, was mortally wounded.

Through the daylight hours of October 17, militia companies from Virginia and Maryland moved into Harpers Ferry. Several raiders were captured or killed. Brown, the remaining raiders, and a handful of hostages were cornered in the Armory's fire enginehouse. Late that evening 90 United States Marines, summoned from Washington, D.C., and joined by Col. Robert E. Lee and Lt. J.E.B. Stuart, entered the Armory yard and replaced the disorganized militia.

At daybreak on October 18, Lt. Israel Green picked a storming party of 12 Marines. After a surrender demand was turned down by Brown, Green and his men battered down the door of the fire enginehouse. In about three minutes the fighting was over. One Marine had been killed, one wounded. Brown, though injured, was taken alive. Of the 19 raiders who had entered Harpers Ferry, ten were killed, five were captured, and four escaped. In addition to Heyward Shepherd and the one Marine, four townspeople were also killed.

Brown, charged for "conspiring with slaves to commit treason and murder," was convicted of this crimes and hanged in nearby Charles Town on December 2, 1859.

John Brown's Fort as it appeared in 1891. (National Park Service photo).

23. Princess Tree. Standing some 40 feet tall, *Paulownia tomentosa*—also known as the royal paulownia, princess tree or empress tree—is a native of southeast Asia and is widely planted in the eastern United States. This tree is best known for its distinctive lavender flowers which bloom in spring. Ovoid, woody capsules enclose masses of tiny winged seeds. The tree was named for Anna, a Russian princess, wife of a king of the Netherlands and daughter of Paul I.

24 & 25. John Brown's Fort (24-present site; 25-original site). The original building was erected in 1848 as the Armory's fire enginehouse and watchman's office. It was in this building that John Brown and several of his followers barricaded themselves during their ill-fated raid of October 16, 17, and 18, 1859.

John Brown's Fort, as the structure was subsequently known, was the only Armory building to escape destruction during the Civil War. In 1891, the fort was dismantled and transported to Chicago where it was displayed at a world exposition. The building, attracting only 11 visitors in ten days, was closed and moved back to Harpers Ferry. From 1895-1909, the fort stood on a farm about three miles upstream along the Shenandoah River. In 1909, on the 50th Anniversary of John Brown's Raid, the fort was moved to the campus of Storer College on Camp Hill. Here the building stood for more that five decades until it was moved to its present location in 1968 by the National Park Service. See also **Camp Hill-Storer College, #8** (page 66).

26. Ferry Lot Reservation. When John Wager, Sr., sold land to the U.S. Government for the Armory in 1796, one of the two parcels of land he retained was the "Ferry Lot Reservation" (see **The Wager Family**, page 33). This $^3/_4$-acre lot, which sat at the confluence of the Potomac and Shenandoah rivers, became a bustling commercial area as the town of Harpers Ferry grew. Businesses here included The Gault House Saloon, the $3^1/_2$-story Wager House Hotel, the Potomac Restaurant, a jewelry store, barber shop, shoe store, drug store, dry goods store, and two clothing stores. The B&O Railroad and Winchester & Potomac Railroad each had depots here as well. Indeed, with all train service and wagon traffic to and from Maryland passing through the "Ferry Lot," this area thrived right up to the Civil War.

But the prosperity of the "Ferry Lot," as well as that of all Harpers Ferry, ended with the Civil War. On February 7, 1862, Union troops burned the buildings here to prevent Confederate sharpshooters from using them for cover. Today, this piece of land is known simply as The Point.

27. Robert Harper's Ferry. In 1761, the Virginia General Assembly granted Robert Harper the right to establish and maintain a ferry across the Potomac River. Harper had in fact been providing ferry service from a small landing here at The Point since 1747, and Peter Stephens before

This 1859 photograph shows the "Ferry Lot Reservation" and the covered railroad and wagon bridge across the Potomac River. (National Park Service photo).

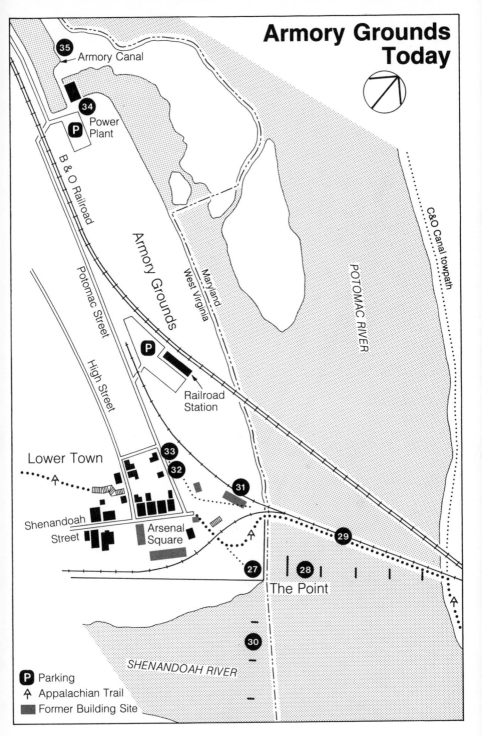

Armory Grounds Today

35 ← Armory Canal

34
P Power Plant

B & O Railroad

Potomac Street

High Street

Armory Grounds

West Virginia

Maryland

C&O Canal towpath

POTOMAC RIVER

P Railroad Station

Lower Town

33
32

31

Shenandoah Street

Arsenal Square

27

28
The Point

29

30

SHENANDOAH RIVER

P Parking
Appalachian Trail
Former Building Site

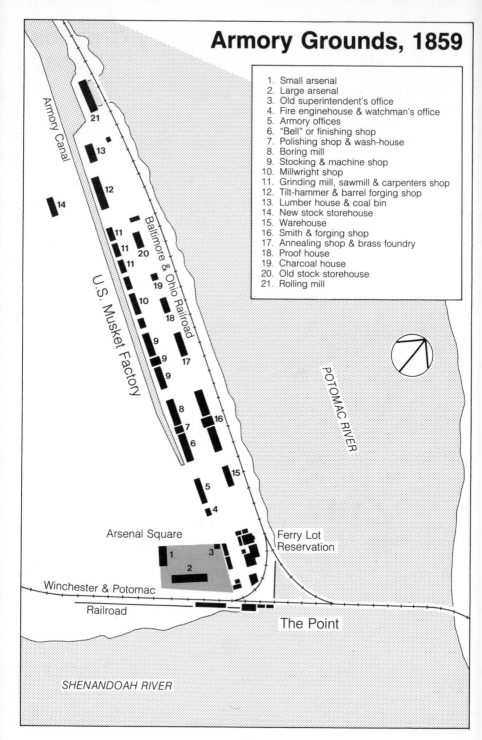

Armory Grounds, 1859

1. Small arsenal
2. Large arsenal
3. Old superintendent's office
4. Fire enginehouse & watchman's office
5. Armory offices
6. "Bell" or finishing shop
7. Polishing shop & wash-house
8. Boring mill
9. Stocking & machine shop
10. Millwright shop
11. Grinding mill, sawmill & carpenters shop
12. Tilt-hammer & barrel forging shop
13. Lumber house & coal bin
14. New stock storehouse
15. Warehouse
16. Smith & forging shop
17. Annealing shop & brass foundry
18. Proof house
19. Charcoal house
20. Old stock storehouse
21. Rolling mill

Armory Canal

Baltimore & Ohio Railroad

U.S. Musket Factory

POTOMAC RIVER

Arsenal Square

Ferry Lot
Reservation

Winchester & Potomac

Railroad

The Point

SHENANDOAH RIVER

him operated a ferry. But now a ferry concession had been awarded, giving Harper exclusive rights to transport foot and wagon traffic across the Potomac River at Harpers Ferry.

The Wager family—heirs of Robert Harper—maintained this ferry concession until 1824, when they began erecting a "handsome double wooden highway bridge, 750 feet from one abutment to the other," across the Potomac River. By the rights inherent in the original ferry concession, the Wager family collected toll from all foot and wagon traffic using their bridge. When the B&O railroad erected a railroad and wagon bridge adjacent to "Wager's Bridge" in 1836, the Wager family was still entitled

---

The Wager Family

When Robert Harper, the town's founder, died in 1782, his estate passed to his niece, Sarah Harper Wager of Philadelphia. Sarah and her husband, John Wager, Sr., never lived in Harpers Ferry. But when the Wager family sold land to the U.S. Government for an armory in 1796, they retained possession of two key parcels. The $3/4$-acre "Ferry Lot Reservation" was situated at the junction of the Potomac and Shenandoah rivers. The "Six-Acre Reservation" extended north from Shenandoah Street between the Stage Coach Inn and Potomac Street. In 1803, John Wager, Jr., inherited these two parcels and moved to Harpers Ferry with his wife Catherine.

As the Armory workforce grew in the early 1800s, both the "Ferry Lot Reservation" and "Six-Acre Reservation" became the commercial heart of Harpers Ferry. The Wager family took full advantage of these centrally located parcels by leasing their tenements and lots at extremely high rates. When the government challenged this monopoly by leasing Armory land to merchants at substantially lower rates, Catherine Wager was furious. She informed the War Department that the U.S. Government had agreed when purchasing land for the Armory in 1796, "that the Person living on her land shall have a monopoly of the mercantile Business of the Place, & that the Persons employed about the Armory, shall be constrained to take all supplies from the Persons occupying her land and tenements at the Ferry."

The Wager commercial monopoly was largely broken up in succeeding decades. Nevertheless, Wager family influence remained strong at Harpers Ferry up until the Civil War. By that time 43 business enterprises were being operated in the Lower Town, serving about 400 Armory workmen and a local population of almost 3,000.

Circa 1882 photo of the Bollman Bridge. Ruins of the Musket Factory's smith and forging shop are in the foreground. (National Park Service photo).

to collect the toll. Finally, in 1839, they conveyed "all rights to take toll, including the rights incident to the original Ferry," to the B&O Railroad. By the same agreement "Wager's Bridge" was torn down.

The large weathered sign painted on the face of Maryland Heights says "Mennens Borate Talcum Toilet Powder." As the story goes, in 1895 or 1896, a German immigrant was hired to paint this sign. Using a mixture of goat's milk and whitewash, the immigrant worked through the summer and was paid $40.

28. B&O Railroad Bridge Ruins. In 1836, the B&O Railroad erected a timber railroad and wagon bridge at Harpers Ferry. A tin roof and weatherboarding were later added to protect the timber spans from the elements. In 1840-1842, a curved span or "Y" was added on the Harpers Ferry end of the bridge to carry the B&O mainline up along the Potomac. In 1850-1852, the timber straight span of this "Y", which carried the tracks of the Winchester & Potomac R.R. up along the Shenandoah, was replaced with a metallic truss. John Brown crossed this bridge when he led his famous raid. Two years later, at 4 a.m. on June 14, 1861, Confederate troops blew it up. Substantial sections of the five masonry piers which carried this bridge still stand in the Potomac River.

During the course of the Civil War, this railroad bridge was destroyed and replaced nine times. After 1862, the B&O Railroad began

West Virginia: The 35th State

After Virginia seceded from the Union in 1861, the loyal residents of the state's western counties met in a series of conventions and voted in turn to "secede" from Virginia. A bill for the admission of West Virginia into the Union was quickly approved by Congress. But the people of Jefferson Country (where Harpers Ferry is located) and neighboring Berkeley County were less enthusiastic about separating from Virginia.

On May 28, 1863, elections were held to determine the issue. In Jefferson Country, which was occupied at the time by Federal forces, 250 voters cast ballots—a small turnout compared to the 1,800 who had cast votes in the 1860 Presidential eiection. Restricted to only two polling places and influenced in a large measure by the presence of Federal troops, voters overwhelmingly chose to join West Virginia. The count was 196 to 1 in Harpers Ferry and 52 to 1 in Shepherdstown. On June 20, 1863, West Virginia became the 35th State by Presidential proclamation.

After the war, Virginia sued West Virginia for the recovery of Jefferson and Berkeley counties, charging fraud in the county elections. But in 1871, the Supreme Court in a 6-3 decision ruled that the allegation of fraud had not been sustained and the question of jurisdiction had been determined by the people of both counties at the polls in 1863.

erecting new iron spans designed by Wendell Bollman. By 1870, this "Bollman Bridge" was completed. Bollman's iron spans carried the B&O mainline until 1894, and continued to serve as a highway bridge into the present century. Floodwaters in 1924 swept away three iron spans, but these were promptly replaced. Twelve years later the record Flood of 1936 destroyed this bridge for good.

29. B&O Railroad Trestle and Footbridge. The original mainline of the B&O ran on top of a 15-foot high stone wall along the Potomac riverfront of the Armory Grounds. In 1892, the railroad began to cut an 800-foot tunnel through Maryland Heights and to erect a new steel railroad bridge. A 20-foot embankment buried part of the old Armory Grounds and carried a new track arrangement. The bridge was opened on April 12, 1894.

A footbridge erected alongside the railroad trestle was completed in 1985, and today carries the Appalachian Trail across the Potomac River.

30. Shenandoah Bridge Ruins. Here in 1882, a new wagon bridge was built across the Shenandoah River. This bridge replaced the old covered bridge 300 yards upstream which had been destroyed during the Civil War (see #2, page 17). The original timber superstructure was swept away in just a few short years by the Flood of 1889. New spans were subsequently erected, however, and the bridge served travelers for more than four decades. The great Flood of 1936, which crested here at $36^1/2$ feet, destroyed this bridge for good.

31. Old B&O Railroad Station. In 1894, the B&O opened a grand new station here, coinciding with the opening of their new bridge across the Potomac River. The new station was built on top of a 20-foot embankment which covered the old Armory Grounds. Only by promising to build this new station was permission obtained from the town of Harpers Ferry to change the mainline track arrangement and cover the old Armory site.

32. White Hall. In 1838-1839, a one-story warehouse was erected here. Frederick A. Roeder purchased the building in 1847, and added the second floor shortly thereafter. "White Hall," as the building was subsequently called, served as a drinking house for Armory employees probably up until the Civil War.

33. Frederick A. Roeder's Store. This building was erected in 1856, and served either as a drinking house or a warehouse up until 1865.

Continue down Potomac Street past the train station about a quarter mile to the Power Plant.

34. Power Plant. In 1854, a Rolling Mill for the Harpers Ferry Armory was erected on this site. Here heavy machinery rolled bar iron into barrel *skelps*, flat pieces of metal used for musket barrels.

In 1884, Thomas Savery of Wilmington, Delaware, purchased the old Armory Grounds, Rifle Factory site, waterfront land, and flowage rights of the Potomac and Shenandoah rivers from the U.S. Government for $200,000. In 1890, on the former site of the Armory's Rolling Mill, Savery erected the Harpers Ferry Paper Company. Water supplied from the Armory Canal drove 12 turbines which in turn powered the mill's machinery (see **Waterpower In The 19th Century**, page 46, and **Paper Manufacture**, page 52). In 1925, this paper mill was totally destroyed by fire.

The present hydro-electric station was built shortly after this fire and stands on the paper mill's original stone foundations.

Circa 1900 photo of the Harpers Ferry Paper Co. (National Park Service photo).

35. Armory Canal. This headrace, which was originally completed in 1801, conveyed water from the Potomac River down to the Musket Factory. A narrow raceway now covered by the railroad embankment continued down along Potomac Street, furnishing water to run the water wheels and turbines of the various Armory workshops.

Between 1830-1860, the U.S. Government spent some $68,000 on rebuilding and repairing the Armory Canal. An 1844 government report describes a sample of the work performed:

> "During the past Season, the canal which supplies the power from the Dam on the Potomac, has received extensive and thorough repairs, in new Head Gates, a Pier head and Ice breakers, and new Gates to the Lock which admits boats with Coal and other supplies for the Armory; indeed, the whole mass of masonry at the head of the Canal and lock, have been renewed and the Canal cleared out."

Return to Hog Alley and continue the walking tour.

36. Frederick A. Roeder's Confectionery. Roeder's original two-story house was built in 1844-1845, and enlarged about five years later. Prior to the Civil War the building served as a confectionery shop where breads, cakes, rolls, and other bakery items were sold.

37. Susan Downey House. The main house was built in 1838-1839. At the time of John Brown's Raid the building was occupied as a shoemaker's shop and private residence. Today the building houses an exhibit on Soldier Life in Harpers Ferry during the Civil War.

George Washington And
The Harpers Ferry Armory

In 1794, Congress approved a bill "for the erecting and repairing of Arsenals and Magazines." Springfield, Massachusetts, was chosen as the site for the first national armory. President George Washington, given wide discretionary powers in executing the legislation, then selected Harpers Ferry for a second national armory.

A report commissioned by the War Department, however, questioned the Harpers Ferry location, pointing out that "there was no ground on which convenient buildings could be placed" and that "no water work would be safe" along the floodprone riverbanks. Washington, who had traveled extensively through the Potomac River valley as a surveyor for Lord Fairfax and later as President of the Patowmack Company, was not impressed. In a letter to the Secretary of War he again recommended the Harpers Ferry site. In 1796, the U.S. Government purchased 118 acres from the Wager family between the Potomac and Shenandoah rivers for the new armory (see **The Wager Family**, page 33).

Construction of the "United States Armory and Arsenal at Harpers Ferry" commenced in 1799. Three years later full-scale production of arms began. Muskets, rifles and, after 1805, pistols were all manufactured at the Harpers Ferry location. By 1810, annual production of arms averaged about 10,000.

Over the next several decades the Armory continued to grow. In 1802, the Armory employed 25 men. By 1859, this workforce had grown to about 400. By this same year the Armory facilities had multiplied to a double row of 20 brick workshops extending 600 yards along the Potomac shoreline. These buildings were known collectively as the "U.S. Musket Factory." Along the Shenandoah River on Lower Hall Island another nine buildings comprised the "U.S. Rifle Factory" (see **John H. Hall**, page 54).

But with the Civil War there came destruction. Confederate troops occupying Harpers Ferry in the spring of 1861 confiscated the Armory's ordnance stock, machinery, and tools. When they withdrew from town on June 14, the Confederates burned the main Armory buildings.

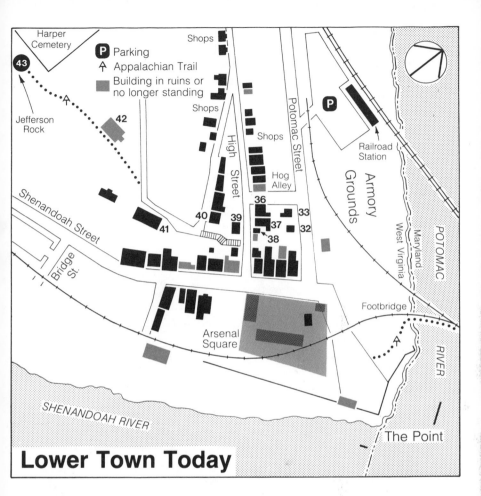

Lower Town Today

38. Alfred Burton Jewelry Store. In 1857, Alfred Burton purchased this small lot for $100. A year later he erected a small jewelry and watch repair store here. The Burton family continued to operate the business until about 1890. In 1956, because of its dilapidated condition, the National Park Service dismantled the original frame building. The structure was re-assembled in 1991, and today houses a replica of Burton's jewelry store.

39. Nichols-Williams Building. This three-story brick building is the fifth structure to occupy the site. Erected by William B. Nichols between 1896-1907, the present building originally served as a grocery store. The Nichols-Williams Building now houses an exhibit on the Civil War

To continue the walking tour, proceed up the Stone Steps.

40. Harper House. In 1775, Robert Harper began to erect this stone house on the side of the hill well above the Lower Town. A scarcity of skilled labor during the American Revolution, however, delayed completion until 1782. Harper, who died in October of that year, never occupied the house. From 1782 to 1803, the building served as the town's only tavern, hosting such prominent guests as Thomas Jefferson and George Washington. The Harper House is the oldest surviving building in Harpers Ferry.

41. St. Peter's Roman Catholic Church. The original church—a one-story building with a tall wooden steeple—was built in 1830-1833 on land donated by the Wager family. The present church building replaced the original structure in 1896.

Robert Harper

Robert Harper was born about the year 1703 in Oxford, England. At the age of 20 Harper emigrated to Philadelphia, where he pursued a career in architecture and mill-wrighting. In 1747, a group of Quakers engaged Harper to erect a meeting house in the Shenandoah Valley near the present site of Winchester.

Traveling through Maryland on his way to the Shenandoah Valley, Harper proceeded to "The Hole" where the Potomac and Shenandoah rivers converged. Here lived Peter Stephens, a trapper and trader who had squatted on this land since 1733. Harper, recognizing the water he could harness to power mills and the traffic he could ferry across the rivers, purchased Stephens' log cabin, corn patch, and ferry equipment. As for the land, Stephens enjoyed only the precarious tenure of squatter's rights. Real ownership was vested in Lord Fairfax, whose vast estate was "bounded by and within the heads" of the Potomac and Rappahannock rivers. This great parcel of land was called the Northern Neck and had originally been set aside by Charles II of England in 1649. In 1688, Lord Culpeper obtained title to the land and in 1736, his grandson Thomas, the sixth Lord Fairfax, came to America as Proprietor of the Northern Neck.

Harper obtained a patent from Fairfax to 125 acres in 1751. Twelve years later the town of "Shenandoah Falls at Mr. Harper's Ferry" was established by an act of the Virginia General Assembly.

Lower Town from Loudoun Heights in 1895. Renovation of St. Peter's Church (center) was begun a year later. (National Park Service photo).

42. St. John's Protestant Episcopal Church. On this site the town's first church, the Free Church, was erected in 1825. Fire destroyed the building two decades later. St. John's Protestant Episcopal Church was built in 1851-1852. During part of the Civil War the church served as barracks for Confederate artillerymen and also served as a hospital. The structure, severely damaged during the war, was rebuilt in 1882. Due to declining membership, however, the church was sold in 1895, and was subsequently abandoned.

43. Jefferson Rock. Several large masses of *Harpers shale*, piled one upon the other, comprise Jefferson Rock (see **Appalachian Geology**, page 81). The uppermost slab originally rested on a natural stone foundation so narrow that one was able to sway the rock back and forth with a gentle push. Because this natural foundation had "dwindled to very unsafe dimensions by the action of the weather, and still more, by the devastations of tourists and curiosity-hunters," four stone pillars were placed under each corner of the uppermost slab sometime between 1855 and 1860.

The name of the rock derives from the tradition that from this point Thomas Jefferson, on October 25, 1783, viewed the Potomac River and its water gap. Jefferson's memorable description of this sight appeared in his *Notes on the State of Virginia*, first published in 1785.

Thomas Jefferson On Harpers Ferry

"The passage of the Patowmac through the Blue Ridge is perhaps one of the most stupendous scenes in Nature. You stand on a very high point of land. On your right comes up the Shenandoah, having ranged along the foot of the mountain a hundred miles to seek a vent. On your left approaches the Patowmac in quest of a passage also. In the moment of their junction they rush together against the mountain, rend it asunder and pass off to the sea. The first glance of this scene hurries our senses into the opinion that this earth has been created in time, that the mountains were formed first, that the rivers began to flow afterwards, that in this place particularly they have been so dammed up by the Blue Ridge of mountains as to have formed an ocean which filled the whole valley; that, continuing to rise, they have at last broken over at this spot and have torn the mountain down from its summit to its base. The piles of rock on each hand, but particularly on the Shenandoah, the evident marks of their disruptions and avulsions from their beds by the most powerful agents in nature, corroborate the impression. But the distant finishing which nature has given the picture is of a very different character. It is a true contrast to the former. It is as placid and delightful as that is wild and tremendous. For the mountains being cloven asunder, she presents to your eye, through the cleft, a small catch of smooth blue horizon, at an infinite distance in that plain country, inviting you, as it were, from the riot and tumult roaring around to pass through the breach and participate in the calm below. Here the eye ultimately composes itself; and that way, too, the road happens actually to lead. You cross the Patowmac above the junction, pass along its side through the base of the mountain for three miles, the terrible precipice hanging in fragments over you, and within about 20 miles reach Frederictown and the fine country around that. This scene is worth a voyage across the Atlantic."

—From *Notes on the State of Virginia,* 1785

Virginius Island, from an 1857 lithograph. Of some three dozen buildings that once stood here, none remain today. (National Park Service photo).

Virginius Island

Allow about one and a half hours for this complete walking tour. The main trail is 1.5 miles long and begins on Shenandoah Street just outside of the Lower Town. Most, but not all, of the site numbers in this guidebook correspond to the numbered stakes along the trail. Many of the ruins on Virginius Island are fragile—please do not walk or climb on them.

1. Armory Stable and Armorer's Dwelling House. On this site, the U.S. Armory erected a stable in 1848-1849. The brick structure, very similar in appearance to the Armory's fire enginehouse and watchman's office which John Brown seized during his ill-fated raid, contained stalls for about six horses.

Across the street sits an old Armorer's dwelling house. To attract skilled craftsmen to come work at the U.S. Armory, the Federal Government initially provided housing for its workers. The front section of this building was erected between 1822-1830. During the 1840s, the building was enlarged into a 2 1/2-story stone structure. Houses such as this were rented out to Armory workmen for about $100 a year.

The trail proceeds along the left bank of the Shenandoah Canal.

2. Virginius Island. You are now standing on Virginius Island. The old canal here was once a river channel which separated the island from the mainland.

In 1824, the "Island in the Shenandoah River near Harpers Ferry," containing about 13 acres, was called Stubblefield's Island. This name derived from James Stubblefield, Superintendent of the Armory, who a year earlier had acquired the property. In 1827, by an act of the Virginia General Assembly, the town of Virginius was established on the island. The property subsequently became known as the Island of Virginius or Virginius Island.

Virginius was a child of the Shenandoah River. Water drawn from the river powered several mills and factories, and a substantial industrial community developed here in the 1800s. By 1859, there were about three dozen buildings on Virginius Island. Among them were a cotton factory, flour mill, sawmill, machine shop, iron foundry, blacksmith shop, chopping mill, and 28 dwellings. But the Shenandoah River could also be harsh. The Flood of 1870 destroyed much of the island's homes and industry, and Virginius never recovered from this blow. Today, nature here has come full circle, reclaiming the land more completely than anywhere else at Harpers Ferry.

3. Shenandoah Canal. In 1785, the Patowmack Company was organized to improve navigation on the Potomac River and its tributaries. George Washington was elected the company's first president, and engineers

Shenandoah Navigation

In 1798, the Virginia General Assembly granted the Shenandoah Company a charter to operate a fleet of flatboat barges on the Shenandoah River. Within ten years, river improvements—including the Patowmack Company's bypass canal at Harpers Ferry—had rendered the Shenandoah and its South Fork navigable upstream to Port Republic, a distance of 160 miles.

The boats that traveled down the Shenandoah were called gundalows—narrow flatbottom barges about nine feet wide by 75 feet long. Principal cargoes were iron, flour, and lumber. Tan-bark, apples, potatoes, corn, tobacco, and brandy were also common river freight. A hundred barrels of flour, weighing about ten tons, usually made a single load. Boatmen poled these loaded gundalows about 35 miles a day, and received from $14 to $18 for the five day trip from Port Republic to Harpers Ferry. Boats that unloaded at Harpers Ferry were usually broken up and sold for lumber, a return trip upstream being impractical.

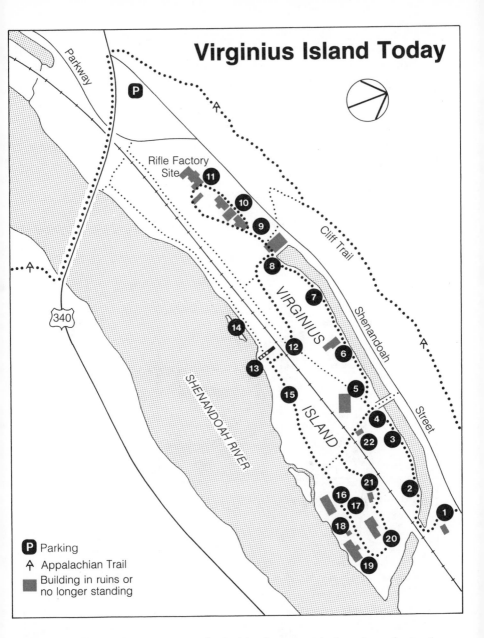

Virginius Island Today

Parkway

P

Rifle Factory Site

11

10

9

8

7

VIRGINIUS

14

12

6

13

5

15

ISLAND

4

22

3

21

2

16

17

1

18

20

19

Cliff Trail

Shenandoah

Street

340

SHENANDOAH RIVER

P Parking

Appalachian Trail

Building in ruins or
no longer standing

proceeded over the next several years to deepen existing river channels
and to construct short bypass canals around dangerous river rapids.

In 1806-1807, the Patowmack Company excavated a 580-yard canal
just above Virginius Island to bypass The Staircase, a rocky series of

(continued on page 49)

Waterpower In The 19th Century

Prior to the advent of the steam engine, water was the principal source of power for the mills and factories of early America. The type of water wheel selected for a mill depended principally on the head of water available—the difference in height between supply water in the mill's headrace and waste water in its tailrace. At Harpers Ferry, where there was a large volume but a low head of water available, breast wheels were most appropriate. These water wheels were fitted with deep buckets or floats—partitions set into slots in the wheel rims—and were turned both by the weight of water carried in the buckets and by the impulse of the water striking the wheel. By 1800, five breast wheels had been installed at the Harpers Ferry Armory.

Middle Breast Wheel, from The Young Mill-wright and Miller's Guide, *by Oliver Evans (1834 edition).*

In 1827, a turbine was invented by Benoit Fourneyron. Water entered this device at the center, flowed outward through an inner ring of fixed guide blades, and struck the moving vanes of an outer runner. The vanes of this outer runner were curved in the opposite direction from the inner guide blades. This reversed the direction of water flow within the turbine, created a reactive force, and thereby extracted more power from the falling water. Two Fourneyron-style turbines, manufactured by E.C. Kilburn & Company of Fall River, Mass., were installed in the Cotton Factory on Virginius Island in about 1850.

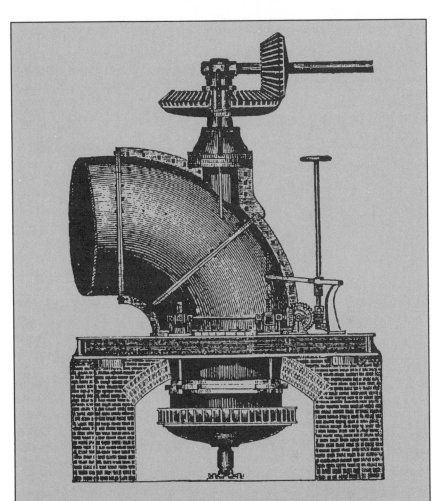

Boyden Turbine, circa 1844. (Courtesy Smithsonian Institution).

Uriah Boyden of Lowell, Mass., patented an improved version of the Fourneyron turbine in 1844. Boyden turbines, which converted more than 80% of the energy available in the falling water into power, replaced the breast wheels of the Musket Factory after 1845.

In 1862, James Leffel of Springfield, Ohio, manufactured a "Double Turbine Water Wheel" which used axial flow discharge vanes beneath inner flow runner vanes. Water entered this turbine from the side through an outer ring of fixed guide blades, struck the moving vanes of an inner runner, and then falling downward

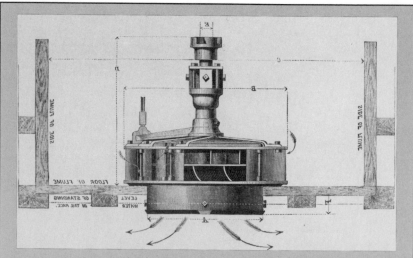

1862 model Leffel turbine. (Ohio Historical Society photo).

struck the axial flow vanes at the bottom of the turbine. This design resulted in a longer, narrower, faster turbine which, according to Leffel, was capable "of yielding from ninety-two to ninety-five per cent. of the power of the water and a greater per cent. than any other wheel heretofore constructed." In 1867, four Leffel turbines were installed in the Child & McCreight flour mill on Virginius Island, where they remain today.

A further improvement in turbine technology was achieved by John B. McCormick in about 1876. By adding spoon-shaped discharge sections to the bottom of a turbine's runner vanes, McCormick found that he could extract more energy from water leaving the wheel. In 1884, the Globe Iron Works of Dayton, Ohio, adopted McCormick's design and patented the "New American Turbine Water Wheel". By making the runner of this turbine a solid, continuous casting without a rivet or bolt, the Globe Iron Works claimed that they had created "a perfect wheel, with even, true, and smooth surfaces, and of unquestioned strength, and which we will guarantee to stand the pressure of any head." New American turbines were installed both in the Shenandoah Pulp Company mill on Virginius Island (see illustration on page 51) and in the Harpers Ferry Paper Company mill.

Falling water remained the primary source of power in America through most of the 19th century. But steam engines were becoming increasingly economical and by 1880, steam finally passed water as the principal source of power in America.

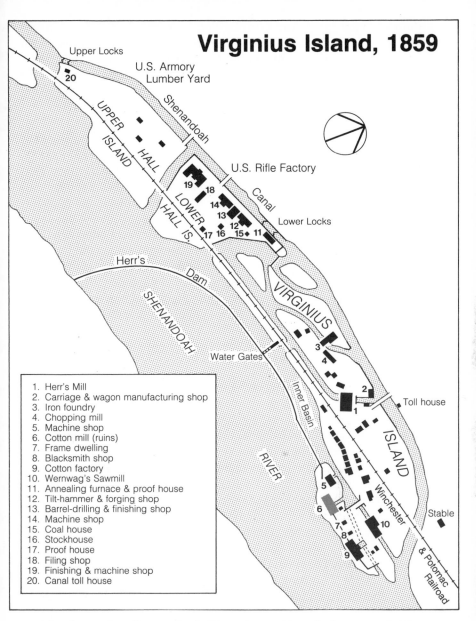

Virginius Island, 1859

Upper Locks

U.S. Armory
Lumber Yard

Shenandoah

UPPER ISLAND HALL

U.S. Rifle Factory

LOWER HALL IS.

Canal

Lower Locks

Herr's

Dam

SHENANDOAH

Water Gates

VIRGINIUS

Inner Basin

ISLAND

Winchester

RIVER

Toll house

Stable

& Potomac
Railroad

1. Herr's Mill
2. Carriage & wagon manufacturing shop
3. Iron foundry
4. Chopping mill
5. Machine shop
6. Cotton mill (ruins)
7. Frame dwelling
8. Blacksmith shop
9. Cotton factory
10. Wernwag's Sawmill
11. Annealing furnace & proof house
12. Tilt-hammer & forging shop
13. Barrel-drilling & finishing shop
14. Machine shop
15. Coal house
16. Stockhouse
17. Proof house
18. Filing shop
19. Finishing & machine shop
20. Canal toll house

rapids along the Shenandoah River here. Two locks were built to
overcome a fall of 17 feet. By deepening existing channels of the river
immediately above and below these locks (including the channel before
you), a waterway over a mile long was created. For several years this
improvement was called the Patowmack Canal. In 1824, the Shenandoah
Company took over the waterway, and it became known as the Shenandoah Canal.

49

4. Randolph Bridge. A wagon bridge here and a railroad bridge adjacent to the old Armory Stable provided residents and factory workers with their only access to Virginius Island. The present bridge is a replica of an 1886 bridge that stood here. The structure is dedicated to former U.S. Senator Jennings Randolph of West Virginia, for his efforts in creating Harpers Ferry National Historical Park.

5. Herr's Mill. The original gristmill here, built in 1824, was one of the earliest industries on Virginius Island. Fire destroyed this mill in 1839, but the following year the Island Flour Mill was erected in its place. This new mill was a substantial stone building 96 feet long by 48 feet wide and 3 1/2 stories tall. Abraham Herr acquired the building in 1848, and it subsequently became known as Herr's Mill.

In October 1861, Herr, who supported the United States when the Civil War erupted, invited Union troops stationed across the Potomac River in Maryland to remove a large quantity of grain from his mill. The 13th Massachusetts and 3rd Wisconsin regiments accepted the offer, and the grain was removed in a few days. Nearby Confederate forces, informed of this action, entered Harpers Ferry a few days later and in retaliation burned Herr's Mill.

Follow the trail to the right alongside the canal.

6. Iron Foundry. In 1835, Hugh Gilleece leased an old tanning mill here and opened an Iron Foundry. Five years later, on June 11, 1840, the *Virginia Free Press* announced that Gilleece had "completed his Chopping Mill, on the Island of Virginius, near the Foundry, where he is prepared to chop Rye and Corn...." Gilleece operated his Iron Foundry and Chopping Mill until 1855, when he sold the properties to Abraham Herr.

The Iron Foundry produced items of every description, including saws, straw cutters, turning lathes, cast iron railings, mill gearing, and even a 3,600-pound iron shaft for the U.S. Armory. One of Gilleece's more popular products was his "Great Western Cook Stove."

7. Harpers Shale. The steep cliffs you see across the canal are comprised of *Harpers shale.* This dark blue-gray rock consists of shales and sandstones which were compressed by geological forces 230 million years ago into a hard metamorphic rock (see **Appalachian Geology**, page 81). Other outcrops of *Harpers shale* occur in the rapids of the Shenandoah and Potomac rivers on either side of Harpers Ferry.

Rock from these cliffs provided sturdy building material for homes and businesses in Harpers Ferry and on Virginius Island. Workers, using basic hand tools and gun powder charges, quarried stone all along Shenandoah Street. The marks of their labors are still visible today.

A pair of New American turbines on a horizontal shaft which operated in the Shenandoah Pulp Company mill. (From an 1892 catalog of The Dayton Globe Iron Works).

8. Shenandoah Pulp Company. In 1887-1888, on the former site of the Shenandoah Canal's lower locks, Thomas Savery of Wilmington, Delaware, erected a large pulp mill. Ten turbines, arranged in pairs in the mill's five massive stone sluiceways, powered wood grinders, rolling machines, and other pulp-making machinery. In the 1920s, Savery's mill had the capacity to produce 15 tons of ground wood pulp daily (see **Paper Manufacture** on the next page). But after several unprofitable years the mill closed down in 1935. A year later the building was leveled by the record Flood of 1936.

Continue alongside the stone retaining wall on your left.

9. Lake Quigley. A large millpond formerly extended behind the Shenandoah Pulp Company mill. The pond was named for John Quigley, who supervised construction of the pulp mill and its waterworks. Water was diverted from the Shenandoah River by a dam about $^3/_4$-mile upstream. The water then entered a long headrace which fed into this millpond. From here the water was admitted through control gates behind the pulp mill as needed to power the turbines and drive the mill's machinery.

Paper Manufacture

During most of the 19th century, the basic raw material for paper was cotton and linen rags. Rag paper was durable and attractive, but as early as the 1850s, the supply of rags could not keep pace with the demand for paper. The idea of using wood as a raw material for paper had been considered early in the 1700s. But it wasn't until about 1858, when German inventor Henry Voelter received a patent from the United States for a new wood-pulp grinder, that a mechanical process for reducing wood to fiber was adopted in this country.

At Harpers Ferry, the Shenandoah Pulp Company used this mechanical process to manufacture ground wood pulp. Logs were floated down to Lake Quigley, and then lifted into the mill by a hoist. Inside the mill, the logs were stripped of their bark, cut into three-foot lengths, and then ground up by a wood-pulp grinder (see illustration below). The pulp fibers were then conveyed through pipes to a wet machine, where they were suspended in water inside an oak vat. Here the pulp fibers were dropped over an endless moving wire cloth which collected the fibers but let the water pass through. From the wire cloth, the pulp passed through pressing rolls and drying cylinders. In this manner, the pulp was rolled into sheets.

Front view of an improved Voelter wood-pulp grinder, patented in 1866.

The newly erected Shenandoah Pulp Company mill appears in this circa 1888 photo of the upper end of Virginius Island. The ruins of Herr's Mill stand in the left foreground. (National Park Service photo).

10. U.S. Rifle Factory. In 1819, the Federal Government awarded a weapons contract to John H. Hall, a Maine inventor who had patented a breech-loading rifle (see **John H. Hall** on the next page). The following year Hall occupied a small frame building on this site. The building, which had been used as a sawmill since the 1790s, became known as Hall's Rifle Works. Over the next two decades, Hall assembled almost 20,000 patent rifles here. Hall left Harpers Ferry in 1840, and production of his rifle was discontinued three years later.

In 1844, the government began tearing down the old frame shops of Hall's Rifle Works and replacing them with a new Rifle Factory. Between 1847-1852, a new finishing shop, tilt hammer shop, and a large machine shop constructed of brick and durable cast-iron framing were all erected here. The Rifle Factory produced standard U.S. Model rifles until the Civil War. In 1861, the Confederacy confiscated 132 machines and thousands of tools and spare parts before setting fire to the entire U.S. Rifle Factory.

11. Turbine Pit. In 1963, archaeologists excavated this turbine pit. This pit and others like it housed the turbines which generated power to run the rolling machines, boring machines, rifling machines, and other

John H. Hall

In 1819, John H. Hall, a New England gunmaker, signed a contract with the War Department to produce 1,000 breech-loading rifles. Under the terms of the contract Hall came to Harpers Ferry, where in February 1820, he occupied a frame building just above Virginius Island. The building became known as Hall's Rifle Works, and the property on which it stood was called Lower Hall Island.

Hall had designed and patented his unique breech-loading rifle in 1811. In the years prior to the 1819 contract, the War Department conducted rigorous tests on the new weapon. Hall's rifle, it was found, took one-third the time to load as a conventional muzzle-loader, was lighter, and had greater accuracy with less recoil.

Hall spent his first years at Harpers Ferry tooling his shop and perfecting precision machinery for producing rifles with inter-changeable parts. Although his first 1,000 patent rifles were not completed until 1825, the War Department was impressed enough with Hall's mechanical innovations to renew his contract. By 1832, Hall had made such progress in mechanizing arms production that Col. George Tolcott wrote:

> "This manufactory has been carried to a greater degree of perfection, as regards the quality of work and uniformity of parts than is to be found anywhere—almost everything is performed by machinery, leaving very little dependent on manual labor."

Hall, using precision machinery for stocking, forging, and cutting components, and an absolute minimum of hand work, had successfully manufactured the first fully interchangeable weapons in America. This was also one of the first examples of assembly line production on a factory-wide scale.

various mechanisms used in the U.S. Rifle Factory. Water was supplied from the Shenandoah Canal through headrace culverts which have long since disappeared.

The trail circles back to the pulp mill. Walk back through the pulp mill ruins, turn right and continue across Virginius Island.

Ruins of the U.S. Rifle Factory after the Civil War. (National Park Service photo).

12. Winchester & Potomac Railroad. On March 14, 1836, the Winchester & Potomac R.R. began regular operations. The line, which extended 32 miles from Harpers Ferry to Winchester, Virginia, bolstered the economy of Virginius Island and soon provided a direct link to Baltimore, Maryland. In the spring of 1861, Confederate forces used this railroad to haul thousands of tons of armory machinery south to Richmond, Virginia, and Fayetteville, North Carolina. Today the line is owned and operated by CSX Corporation.

The underpass here formerly carried water from the Shenandoah River to mills in the center of Virginius Island.

13. Intake Arches. These three brick-lined arches were erected in 1850. When control gates on the arches were raised, water from the Shenandoah River was admitted into an Inner Basin and then distributed to the various water-powered mills on Virginius Island.

Walk through the Intake Arches to see the remains of Herr's Dam.

14. Herr's Dam. The line of carefully laid stones, held together by a stubborn row of trees, is the only extant section of Herr's Dam. Originally built in 1850, the dam extended across the Shenandoah River and diverted water through the Intake Arches to the Inner Basin. In 1867, and again after the Flood of 1870, the dam was rebuilt by the firm of Child &

Rocks, Trees, And Water

The moist, loamy soils of Virginius Island sustain a healthy forest of bottomland hardwoods. Sycamore, with its distinctive whitish-brown bark that peels in thin, irregular patches, is the largest of these riverside trees. White ash is especially strong and resilient, and its wood is often used to make baseball bats, hockey sticks, and shovel handles. Silver maple, boxelder, yellow poplar, and mulberry are also common to these riverside soils.

Bird life in this forest is varied and abundant. The wood thrush is distinctive for its song, which consists of a loud series of flute-like phrases ending in a softer guttural trilling. The cardinal is common here and is the West Virginia State Bird. The red-winged blackbird, which frequents the riverbanks, is named for the bright red shoulder patches which occur on the male.

The shallow waters of the Shenandoah River provide a warm habitat for a variety of fish, birds, and insects. Ledges of *Harpers shale* form a series of rapids here called The Staircase. Between these ledges, in small eddies and shallow pools, spottail, spot fin, rosyface shiners, and insect fauna such as mayflies and caddis flies thrive. These small fish and insects in turn attract smallmouth bass, channel catfish, and sunfish.

A variety of birds frequent The Staircase. Mallards and wood ducks commonly feed on insects and aquatic vegetation. The great blue heron, which stands over three feet tall, has a spear-like bill, long legs, and a long neck well suited to snatching fish from the river. The belted kingfisher, which also feeds on fish, has a long pointed bill and a distinctive blue crest on its head. Its call consists of a loud high rattle.

McCreight, who had purchased the former holdings of Abraham Herr on Virginius Island. Following the Flood of 1889, the dam was abandoned.

15. Inner Basin. Water drawn from the Shenandoah River was stored in a basin or millpond here before being distributed to the headraces of the mills on Virginius Island. A stone wall or dike separated the basin from the river. Parts of this stone wall are still visible. Silt, deposited by frequent inundation of the area, has completely filled in the basin.

16. Cotton Mill. In 1849, the Harpers Ferry & Shenandoah Manufacturing Company opened a new four-story brick cotton mill here. The *Virginia Free Press* had this to say about the "Valley Cotton Factory" on August 2, 1849:

This circa 1882 photo shows Herr's Dam and the three intake arches at the upper end of Virginius Island. (National Park Service photo).

"This factory is capable of manufacturing 400 lbs. of Cotton yarn, 1,100 lbs. of Batting, and 50 lbs. of Candle wick per day. The Machinery consists of seven Carders, four Spinning frames (called the Danforth Cap Frame), two Reels.... This establishment employs some of the best and most experienced hands now in this country—some of them from establishments in Manchester, England."

The mill, however, soon fell into financial trouble. On April 8, 1852, the Harpers Ferry & Shenandoah Manufacturing Company advertised the sale of its assets. Ten days later, the devastating Flood of 1852 swept the building away, and it has remained in ruins ever since.

17. Water Tunnels. These stone-lined tunnels were part of an elaborate water supply system created to power the machinery in the Cotton Factory (see below). When water admitted from the Inner Basin passed through these tunnels, the combination of gravity and pressure increased the force of the water. This resulted in more power being generated when the water passed through the Cotton Factory's turbines.

18. Blacksmith Shop. Built in 1834, this small building was destroyed by the Flood of 1870.

19. Cotton Factory. Between 1847-1848, the Harpers Ferry & Shenandoah Manufacturing Company erected a four-story "Brick Factory Building, of the most permanent character," here on Virginius Island. The building was fitted with gas lights, heated by steam with pipes, and was equipped with the latest in cotton machinery. Eighteen carding engines, three drawing frames, 18 spinning frames with a total of 2,376 spindles, and 97 looms were powered by two brand new iron turbines (see **Cotton Manufacture** on the next page).

In 1852, the Harpers Ferry & Shenandoah Manufacturing Company went bankrupt, but new owners continued to operate the factory up until the Civil War.

In 1867, the firm Child & McCreight of Springfield, Ohio, purchased this building and converted it into a flour mill. Four new Leffel Double Turbine Water Wheels, which together produced about 300 horsepower, drove ten pair of burr-stones with a capacity of 500 barrels of flour a day (see **Waterpower In The 19th Century**, page 46). The mill operated for 22 years until the Flood of 1889 forced the company into bankruptcy. The building was abandoned, and the last of its brick walls were brought down by the Flood of 1936.

1900 photograph of the abandoned Cotton Factory. (National Park Service photo).

Cotton Manufacture

In 1793, Eli Whitney invented a Cotton Gin which mechanically separated seed from fiber. This machine was subsequently refined into several specialized units. In the Cotton Factory on Virginius Island a Cotton Opener and Cleaner were used in combination with a Picker to clean dust and burrs and to separate seed from fiber.

The cleaned cotton was passed through several cylinders of a carding engine. Wire teeth fitted on these cylinders combed out the cotton fibers, rolled the cotton into several layers called the *lap*, and then combed this *lap* into a thick rope or *sliver*.

On a drawing frame this loose, irregular rope or *sliver* was stretched and tightened into a continuous thread called a *roving*. On a spinning frame spools of *roving* passed to an equal number of spindles. The *roving*, held firmly by a clasp, was drawn and simultaneously twisted under tension on these spindles. This action produced a fine, soft yarn ready for weaving.

Yarn went from the spinning frame to a power loom. Here a *flying shuttle* moved swiftly from side to side, carrying the *weft* (the horizontal thread) back and forth across the *warp* as the odd and even threads were alternately lifted. The final product was a finely woven cotton cloth.

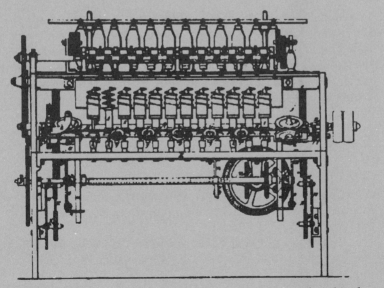

Danforth Cap Frame, a spinning machine patented in 1841 and used in the Cotton Mill on Virginius Island. (U.S. Patent Office).

20. Wernwag's Sawmill. A large frame sawmill, measuring 100 feet by 36 feet, was erected in this vicinity in about 1824 by Lewis Wernwag. Wernwag was a bridge builder and inventor of some reputation. In October 1824, he erected a wooden highway bridge across the Potomac River for the Wager family, and four years later he rebuilt the Armory Dam for the U.S. Government.

In Sept. 1846, the *Virginia Free Press* described the mill as a "double Saw Mill, of Crosbey's Patent, together with two carriages, Straps, and all the Irons belonging to said Mills, and two Circular Saws, of about 24 inches in diameter, and all the Straps belonging thereto."

The Sawmill was leveled by the Flood of 1870.

21. Foundation Ruins. A large 3 1/2-story house once rested on these foundations. Of some 28 dwelling houses that stood on Virginius Island in 1859, almost no remains can be found today. Virtually every small building and quite a few large ones were swept away by the Flood of 1870.

22. The Child's House. Jonathan and Emily Child moved into a large house here in 1867. Jonathan and his partner John McCreight had just purchased the former holdings of Abraham Herr on Virginius Island. Three years later, during the Flood of 1870, the Childs would have the experience of their life. Emily Child described this flood in a letter to her mother and sister:

"We had no idea of the danger until it was too late to escape from the Island. Last Friday towards evening the water commenced rising rapidly. Before two hours every way of escape and all hope of rescue was cut off from us. So we were compelled to stay within the crumbling walls which sheltered us from the terrible water which seethed and dashed around us. There were two bridges connecting the Island with the mainland, one wooden one near our house and the railroad bridge. So violent was the water that these were torn to fragments and carried away...."

The Child family was lucky. By the time the floodwaters receded, 42 lives had been lost and untold property damage inflicted. It was a blow from which Virginius Island would not recover.

You can follow the trail back along the near side of the canal to the start, or cross the Randolph Bridge and walk back along Shenandoah Street.

The Lockwood House in 1958. The third floor and its mansard roof were subsequently removed during the building's restoration. (National Park Service photo).

Camp Hill-Storer College

Begin this walking tour at Jefferson Rock just above St. Peter's Roman Catholic Church. Allow 1-2 hours for this complete walking tour.

1. Harper Cemetery. This four-acre tract of land, possessing a panoramic view of the Potomac and Shenandoah rivers and Blue Ridge Mountains, was set aside as a cemetery by Robert Harper's will, following his death in 1782. Near the cemetery's lower end, enclosed by a low stone wall, lie the gravesites of Harpers and several of his Wager family relatives (see **The Wager Family**, page 33). Many of the headstones, including Robert Harper's, have been severely damaged and are unrecognizable today.

Continue up the hill through the cemetery to the Lockwood House.

2. Lockwood House. Erected in 1847-1848, the original structure was a one-story house which served as the Armory Paymaster's Quarters. A second floor was added in 1858. Armory records referred to the structure simply as Building No. 32. In 1864, Union General Henry Lockwood used the house as his headquarters, and later General Philip H. Sheridan occupied this building.

As the Civil War came to a close, the Ordnance Department, which owned the building, loaned it to the Reverend Dr. Nathan Cook Brackett of the Free Will Baptist Home Mission, an abolitionist group dedicated to educating black freedmen. Brackett established his residence, mission headquarters, and a Freewill Baptist primary school here.

The Lockwood House, as the building became commonly known, had suffered considerable damage during the Civil War. The Rev. A.H. Morrell, an associate of Brackett's, recalled that the building "was little but battered walls, only partially supplied with windows, and roof riddled by shells and cannon balls."

On October 2, 1867, with the help of a generous contribution by John Storer of Sanford, Maine, Brackett opened the "Storer Normal School" in the Lockwood House (see **Storer College**, page 64). Two years later, in December 1869, the government transferred ownership of the Lockwood House and three other former Armory properties to the trustees of Storer College.

In 1877 and again in 1879, the trustees of the college appropriated funds to add a third story with ten new rooms and a mansard roof to the building. These additions were completed in 1883. Gradually, however, as Storer College erected new classroom buildings and dormitories, the Lockwood House fell into disuse. When the college closed in 1955, the building was left in considerable disrepair.

Acquired by the National Park Service in 1960, the Lockwood House has been carefully restored to its Civil War era appearance.

3. Brackett House. This structure, identified in Armory records as Building No. 31, was erected in 1858 and served as quarters for the Armory superintendent's clerk. In December 1869, the house was conveyed by the government to the trustees of Storer College. Subsequently, the building provided housing for students and faculty. Today, the building houses the National Park Service's Curators of Reference Services (the park's furnishing plan team).

The building is named for the Reverend Dr. Nathan Cook Brackett of Phillips, Maine, a key figure in the formation of Storer College, and the school's first principal. As an agent of the Free Will Baptist Home Mission, Brackett came to the Shenandoah Valley in October 1865, where he set about establishing freedmen's schools in Jefferson and Berkeley counties, West Virginia.

4. Morrell House. Erected in 1858, this building served as quarters for the Armory paymaster's clerk, and was officially identified as Building No. 30. In December 1869, along with the Lockwood House, Brackett House, and Armory superintendent's house (see below), this building was

Camp Hill-Storer College

⚐ Appalachian Trail
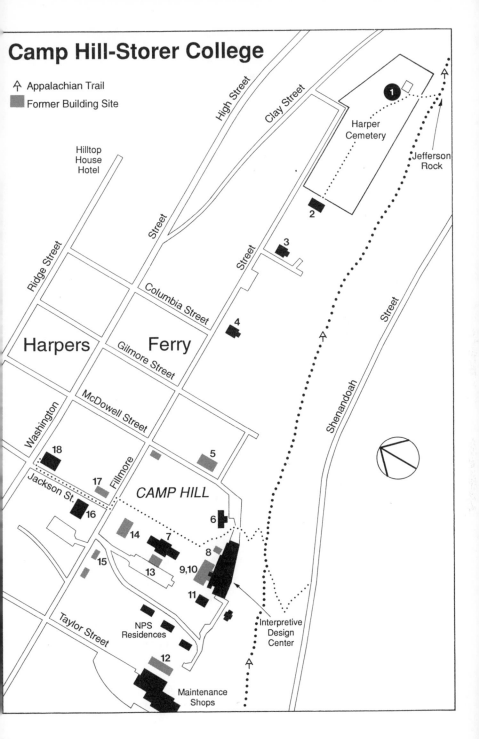
■ Former Building Site

High Street

Clay Street

Harper Cemetery

Jefferson Rock

Hilltop House Hotel

Street

Ridge Street

Columbia Street

Street

Street

Harpers   Ferry

Gilmore Street

Shenandoah   Street

McDowell Street

Washington

Fillmore

18

5

Jackson St.

17

CAMP HILL

16

14   7

6

15

8

13   9,10

11

NPS Residences

Taylor Street

12

Interpretive Design Center

Maintenance Shops

Storer College

In 1865, the Shenandoah Valley was home for some 30,000 black freedmen, many of whom had congregated at Harpers Ferry where Union forces afforded some measure of protection and support. J.H. McKenzie, a Freedmen's Bureau officer, wrote on March 31, 1866:

"In Jefferson County there are many helpless destitute persons both Freedmen and Refugees.... There has been considerable suffering for the want of sufficient clothing, but they have been relieved in a measure by the Rev. Mr. Brackett."

The Reverend Dr. Nathan Cook Brackett, serving as an agent of the Free Will Baptist Home Mission, had arrived in Harpers Ferry in October 1865. Within a year he had established a mission headquarters and a Freewill Baptist primary school in the Lockwood House on Camp Hill.

Brackett's tireless efforts to establish freedmen's schools in the area inspired the generous contribution of philanthropist John Storer of Sanford, Maine, who offered $10,000 for the establishment of a school in the South. The donation was offered on the condition that the school be open to all regardless of sex, race or religion, and that the monies he offered be matched by the Free Will Baptists.

Because of its large freedmen's population, the historic significance of John Brown's Raid, and the availability of abandoned Armory buildings, Harpers Ferry was chosen as the site of the school. On October 2, 1867, "Storer Normal School" was opened in the Lockwood House.

In March 1868, the school was granted a charter by the State of West Virginia, and in December 1869, the government conveyed the Lockwood House and three other abandoned Armory buildings on Camp Hill to the school's trustees. In 1872, the school graduated its first class—eight students with credentials to teach in freedmen's schools. It was not, however, until 1938 that Storer at last became a degree-granting college.

In 1954, the landmark school desegregation decision handed down by the Supreme Court in *Brown v. The Board of Education* was the final blow to Storer College. Financial troubles and a dwindling enrollment forced the school to close one year later.

On July 14, 1960, the grounds and buildings of Storer College, along with John Brown's Fort, were incorporated into Harpers Ferry National Monument.

transferred by the government to the trustees of Storer College. Subsequently, the house provided accommodations for school teachers as well as dormitory space for 12-20 girls. In 1960, the building was incorporated into Harpers Ferry National Historical Park, and today houses the Superintendent's office and Park Administration.

The house derived its name from the Reverend Alexander H. Morrell of Bath, Maine, who resided here from 1870-1881. Morrell, a highly regarded New England pastor, was summoned to Harpers Ferry in the Fall of 1867 by the Free Will Baptist Home Mission in order to strengthen the denomination's spiritual forces in the area.

Morrell's first missionary tour, however, was cut short by bad health. A second missionary tour to Harpers Ferry, spanning more than ten years—from 1870-1881—brought Morrell much closer to the Storer College community. He wrote that "he knew every student, became acquainted with the state of mind of each, and every one was conscious that he was thought of and prayed for."

Morrell became so attached to the college that, after a brief missionary tour in Rhode Island, he resigned his pastorate in 1885 to enter upon the agency of Storer College, "to see the school endowed and its permanency secured...." Unfortunately, Morrell again became ill and died on December 24, 1885. He was buried three days later in Harpers Ferry.

5. Gymnasium. Around 1923, the Robinson Barn, which stood on this site, was converted into a basketball court. The barn had previously been used for Storer College's husbandry and gardening activities. The building was demolished shortly after 1960.

6. Permelia Eastman Cook Hall. Erected by Storer College in 1940, this three-story stone building housed a new physics laboratory and home economics department. The building was rehabilitated in 1962, and today houses a dormitory for visiting National Park Service personnel.

7. Anthony Hall. The right wing of this building, identified in Armory records as Building No. 25, was erected in 1847-1848 and served as the Armory superintendent's house. The building became commonly known as the Commanding Officer's Quarters. After the Battle of Antietam, the house served as headquarters for Second Corps of the Army of the Potomac, and hosted President Abraham Lincoln as an overnight guest on October 1, 1862.

In December 1869, the government conveyed the building and surrounding property to the trustees of Storer College. The building was subsequently called Anthony Hall, or Old Anthony Hall, and replaced the Lockwood House as the school and mission headquarters.

Commanding Officer's Quarters in 1862. The 5th New York Heavy Artillery is encamped in front of the building. (National Park Service photo).

In 1882, Mr. Lewis W. Anthony of Providence, Rhode Island, in memory of his deceased children, contributed more that $5,000 toward the construction of a large new addition to the building. On Memorial Day, 1882, Anthony Memorial Hall was officially dedicated. The new two-story brick building contained the main library, a small museum, music rooms, a chapel hall, the Bowen Lecture Room, science laboratories, and administrative offices.

Damaged by fire in 1928, Anthony Hall was rebuilt in 1930. The building was rehabilitated by the National Park Service in 1963, and presently houses the Mather Training Center.

8. John Brown's Fort. For over 50 years, from 1909 to the mid 1960s, John Brown's Fort stood on this site. The building housed a small museum, and served as an important symbol to the Storer College community of the struggle black Americans had faced to win their freedom.

Acquired by the National Park Service in 1960, the building was disassembled and moved back to the Lower Town in 1968. See also **The Lower Town, 24 & 25**, page 29.

John Brown's Fort had indeed followed a curious path since first being removed from the Lower Town in 1891. In 1894, after a brief and unsuccessful stay in Chicago at the World's Columbian Exposition, a Miss Kate Field raised enough money to bring the building back to Harpers Ferry. The fort was rebuilt on a remote lot about three miles outside of town, where it was relatively inaccessible to visitors. Miss Field had hoped to use the fort as a focal point for creating a national park, but with her untimely death, the property fell into the hands of a farmer with little interest in the historic structure.

When the trustees of Storer College learned that this farmer was neglecting the building and was planning to use it for storage, they raised $2,000 to purchase the fort. In 1909, on the occasion of the 50th anniversary of John Brown's Raid, the building was moved to the Storer College campus.

9. Lincoln Hall. Between 1870-1871, the Freedmen's Bureau made $4,000 available to Storer College for the construction of Lincoln Hall. This three-story frame dormitory, which contained 34 double rooms for boys, burned to the ground on April 12, 1909.

10. Brackett Hall. A four-story grey stone building was erected here in 1909-1910 on the former site of Lincoln Hall. Originally known as New Lincoln Hall, this building contained a Y.M.C.A. room, a superintendent's flat, a dining room and kitchen for the school's men's club, a general reception room, and a gymnasium. Dormitory accommodations were also provided for about 100 students. In 1938, the building was renamed Brackett Hall. The building was demolished in 1962, and today the National Park Service's Interpretive Design Center stands on this site.

John Brown's Fort and Brackett Hall on the campus of Storer College. (National Park Service photo).

Remembering John Brown

On the occasion of the 14th Anniversary of Storer College—May 30, 1881—Frederick Douglass delivered a memorable oration on the subject of John Brown in front of Anthony Hall. Especially notable was the presence among the platform guests of Andrew Hunter, the District Attorney of Charles Town who had prosecuted Brown and secured his conviction. Douglass' address was subsequently published, with the proceeds of its sale earmarked for the endowment of a John Brown Professorship at Storer College.

Twenty-five years later, Storer College hosted another memorable gathering. On August 17, 1906, nearly 100 people gathered at the college to commemorate the 100th anniversary of John Brown's birth and the 50th jubilee of his bloody skirmish with pro-slavery settlers at Osawatomie, Kansas. The group hiked to the site of John Brown's Fort, over a mile away on the Murphy Farm, where they recalled the events of John Brown's Raid and sang "The Battle Hymn of the Republic."

Later in the day, in front of Anthony Hall on the grounds of Storer College, the group gathered to hear a number of prominent black speakers, among them Lewis Douglass—son of Frederick Douglass—Henrietta Leary Evans—whose brother and nephew had fought and died beside John Brown—and W.E.B. DuBois.

The people celebrating this John Brown's Day observance were in fact delegates to the convention of the Niagara Movement, a one-year-old black civil rights organization that had been formed the previous summer at Niagara Falls. Too militant for the likes of Booker T. Washington, an avowed non-militant, the Niagara Movement did not enjoy united black support, and disappeared within a few short years. But in its glorification of John Brown and its demand for racial equality, the Niagara Movement made a lasting contribution to black history.

11. Lewis W. Anthony Industrial Building. Erected in 1903, this three-story stone building originally housed a blacksmith shop, carpenter shop, store room, and office. In 1929, the building was converted into the school's library. When Storer College closed in 1955, this library held some 15,000 volumes. Today the building houses the National Park Service's Reference Service Library.

12. Science Building. Constructed in 1947 with federal funds, this structure housed biology, chemistry, and physics laboratories. The building was demolished by the National Park Service after 1960.

13. DeWolf Industrial Building. A three-story stone structure containing a demonstration kitchen, agricultural and botany classrooms, and a physical sciences laboratory was erected here in 1891. The building was demolished in 1962.

14. Myrtle Hall. When an initial effort to raise funds for a new women's dormitory at Storer College faltered, the Women's Missionary Society stepped in to spearhead a renewed fundraising drive. Led by Frances Steward Mosher, the needed funds were finally raised, and Myrtle Hall was completed in 1879. The four-story brick building contained 35 dormitory rooms for 60 women and several teachers. A laundry room, library, and reading room were also housed here.

The building's name derived from a Sabbath School paper, *The Myrtle*, edited by Mrs. Mosher. The building subsequently became known as Mosher Hall. In 1962, the building was torn down.

15. Sinclair Cottage. One of several small cottages purchased by Storer College between 1912-1923, and used to house students and teachers. Most of these houses were demolished by the National Park Service in 1962.

16. Curtis Freewill Baptist Church. This two-story red brick church was erected in 1894, and named in honor of the Reverend Silas P. Curtis of New Hampshire. The first floor originally contained a kitchen, classroom, library, and vestry room. The upper floor contained the church auditorium.

17. President's House. In 1909, a two-story frame house was erected here as the residence of the Storer College president. The building later burned down, and the president and his family moved into the Brackett House.

18. Appalachian Trail Conference Headquarters. Since 1925, the ATC has spearheaded an unprecedented cooperative effort among hard-working volunteers, generous benefactors, and far-sighted government agencies to develop, protect, and maintain the Appalachian Trail. The ATC currently has an over-all membership of some 21,000 individuals and families, three dozen companies, and about 70 clubs and organizations. Hiking information, trail guides, and maps are all available at the ATC headquarters.

Maryland Heights

Allow about three and a half hours for this complete walking tour. By foot, you can begin this tour at The Point in Harpers Ferry. By car, take Keep Tryst Road off of U.S. Route 340, turn right on Sandy Hook Road, pass through Sandy Hook, and drive under the two railroad trestles to the first open parking lot on the right.

1. Appalachian Trail. Benton Mackaye, a naturalist from Massachusetts, first proposed "An Appalachian Trail" in 1921. The following year the first mile of the Trail was cut and marked in the Palisades Interstate Park in New York State. By 1937, the project was initially completed. Today, this popular recreational footpath extends over 2,000 miles from Maine to Georgia, traversing 14 states, two national parks, and eight national forests.

2. Bridge Ruins. In 1836, the B&O Railroad erected a timber railroad and wagon bridge across the Potomac River here. This structure was subsequently enclosed with a tin roof and weatherboarding to protecting the timber spans from the elements. John Brown used this bridge when he led his famous raid in 1859. Two years later—at 4 a.m. on June 14, 1861—Confederate troops blew it up.

The Bollman Bridge from The Point prior to 1924. (National Park Service photo).

70

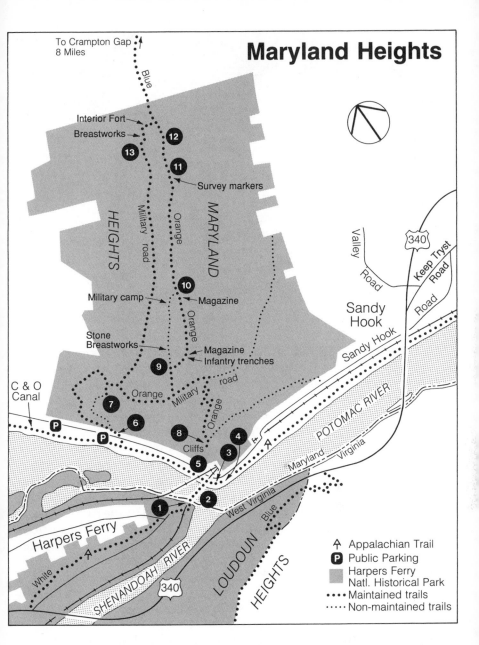

Maryland Heights

To Crampton Gap
8 Miles

Blue

Interior Fort
Breastworks

13
12

11
Survey markers

HEIGHTS

MARYLAND

Military road

Orange

Military camp
Magazine

10

Orange

Stone
Breastworks
Magazine
Infantry trenches

9

Orange
Military road

Orange

C & O
Canal

7

Orange

P

6

8

P

Cliffs

5

4

3

2

1

Harpers Ferry

White

SHENANDOAH RIVER

340

Valley Road

340

Keep Tryst Road

Road

Sandy Hook

Sandy Hook

POTOMAC RIVER

Maryland
Virginia

West Virginia

Blue

LOUDOUN

HEIGHTS

Appalachian Trail
P Public Parking
Harpers Ferry
Natl. Historical Park
•••• Maintained trails
••••• Non-maintained trails

After 1862, the B&O Railroad began erecting new iron spans designed by Wendell Bollman. By 1870, this "Bollman Bridge" was completed. Bollman's iron spans carried the B&O mainline until 1894, and continued to serve as a highway bridge for another four decades. The record Flood of 1936 destroyed this bridge for good.

71

1876 photo of Lock 33 and the Salty Dog Saloon. (National Park Service photo).

3. C&O Canal Towpath. The towpath beneath you once bore the hoofs of mules towing 92-foot barges along the old Chesapeake & Ohio Canal. This property first came under Federal ownership when the U.S. Government purchased it in 1938 from the receivers of the defunct C&O Canal Company. Ten years later Congress studied the feasibility of using the canal and towpath as a route for a vehicular parkway.

But conservationists, led by Supreme Court Justice William O. Douglas, opposed the parkway. In 1954, Douglas wrote a letter urging editors of a local newspaper which supported the parkway to accompany him on a hike down the entire length of the canal. In his letter, he described this natural sanctuary "...not yet marred by the roar of wheels and the sound of horns.... The stretch of 185 miles of country from Washington to Cumberland, Maryland, is one of the most fascinating and picturesque in the Nation."

Through the efforts of Douglas and fellow conservationists, the parkway plan was abandoned. On Jan. 8, 1971, the Chesapeake & Ohio Canal National Historical Park was created by an Act of Congress.

4. Shenandoah River Lock. Covered today with silt and with part of a stone wall built to protect the old canal, little evidence remains of this abandoned river lock. Here boats traveling down the Shenandoah River or taking on freight at Harpers Ferry were admitted into the C&O Canal. In 1836, a tow walk was built on the downstream side of the original B&O railroad and wagon bridge, permitting barges to be towed across the

Chesapeake & Ohio Canal

In the early 1800s, America turned its attention to building artificial canals as a means of providing cheap, reliable transportation. In 1817-1825, the Erie Canal was built in New York State. A year later the Pennsylvania Mainline Canal was begun. On July 4, 1828, construction commenced on the Chesapeake & Ohio Canal as President John Quincy Adams ceremoniously turned the first spadeful of earth near Little Falls.

The C&O Canal, which ultimately extended 184.5 miles between Washington, D.C., and Cumberland, Maryland, along the north bank of the Potomac River, was completed in 1850. Seventy-four locks, each with a lift of about eight feet, raised the canal a total of 605 feet on its course westward. Seven stone aqueducts carried canal and towpath across large tributary streams. Paw Paw Tunnel, carved 3,117 feet through solid rock, was the canal's most ambitious enterprise. Here canal and towpath traveled one mile where the Potomac, in gargantuan loops, travels six.

The canal's primary freight was coal, corn, wheat, and flour, carried on mule-drawn barges some 92 feet long. But large construction cost overruns, seasonality of trade (the canal did not operate in winter), frequent damage from flooding, and increasing competition from the B&O Railroad drove the canal into financial straights. The Flood of 1924 closed the canal for good.

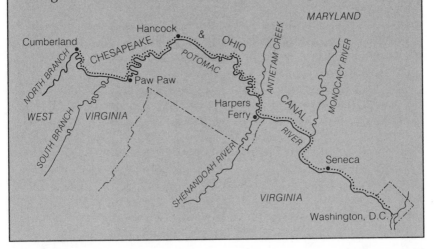

Potomac River to and from this lock. But the tow walk was dismantled five years later and boats were subsequently poled by hand across the river. The lock gradually fell into disuse and, after the Flood of 1889, a tall stone wall was erected here to protect the canal from high water.

Stonewall Jackson Captures Harpers Ferry

In a daring move, Robert E. Lee divided his Army of Northern Virginia on September 10, 1862, at Frederick, Maryland. The corps of James Longstreet and D.H. Hill advanced toward Hagerstown in preparation for an invasion of Pennsylvania. Maj. Gen. Thomas "Stonewall" Jackson, with 32,000 men, was ordered to capture Harpers Ferry and secure Confederate supply lines from the Shenandoah Valley.

Lee divided Jackson's force into three wings. One wing, under Jackson's direct command, advanced from Frederick to Boonsboro, crossed the Potomac River at Williamsport, captured Martinsburg, and came up behind Harpers Ferry from the southwest.

A second wing, commanded by Brig. Gen. John G. Walker, crossed the Potomac River at Point of Rocks 10 miles downstream from Harpers Ferry and proceeded to Loudoun Heights. Col. Dixon S. Miles, who commanded over 14,000 Union troops garrisoning Harpers Ferry, had neglected to post any men or artillery on these heights, considering them to be well within range of Federal gunners on Maryland Heights. Walker moved a battery of artillery up onto Loudoun Heights and, on September 14, exchanged the first artillery fire with Union guns.

A third wing was commanded by Maj. Gen. Lafayette McLaws. McLaws understood the topography around Harpers Ferry well. "So long as Maryland Heights was occupied by the enemy," he wrote, "Harper's Ferry could never be occupied by us. If we gained possession of the heights, the town was no longer tenable to them."

McLaws ordered two infantry brigades to advance south along the crest of Elk Ridge—the northern extension of Maryland Heights. On September 13, these Confederates drove 4,600 Union defenders off the mountain in a fierce skirmish. One day later, McLaws opened fire on Harpers Ferry with four guns.

Confederate artillery fire upon Harpers Ferry was effective and demoralizing. Col. William H. Trimble of the 60th Ohio wrote that there was "not a place where you could lay the palm of your hand and say it was safe." The Union garrison, surrounded and unable to defend itself, surrendered on the morning of September 15.

Jackson captured 12,693 men at Harpers Ferry—the largest single capture of Union troops during the entire war. Also seized were 13,000 arms and 73 pieces of artillery.

The view from Maryland Heights in the immediate aftermath of the 1936 flood. (National Park Service photo).

5. Lock 33. This lift lock was completed in November 1833. The lock walls were constructed primarily of Virginia flint, hauled by wagon across the Shenandoah and Potomac rivers from a quarry a mile and a half away. A frame lockhouse formerly stood on top of the masonry wasteway culvert alongside the lock. The white-washed building ruins on Harpers Ferry Road are the remains of the Salty Dog Saloon, a seedy tavern reputed to be one of the roughest spots on the old canal.

Continue along the towpath until you come to a footbridge. Cross over to Harpers Ferry Road and begin a steep climb on the orange-blazed Grant Conway Memorial Trail.

6. Military Road. Realizing the importance Maryland Heights played in successfully defending Harpers Ferry from Confederate attack during the Civil War, General George B. McClellan directed Union engineers in September 1862 to ring the mountain with formidable defenseworks. The following month work commenced on improving existing fortifications and on erecting substantial new ones.

The Grant Conway Memorial Trail begins ascending Maryland Heights here on an old military road. This road and others further up the mountain were built during the Civil War and used by Union troops garrisoning the fortifications on Maryland Heights.

7. Naval Battery. The Naval Battery was erected on May 27-29, 1862, by Federal troops occupying Harpers Ferry. The battery consisted of heavy guns normally used for seacoast operations—two nine-inch Dahlgrens, one 50-pounder gun, and four light 12-pounder howitzers. These guns were originally manned by a naval detachment.

The large hole in the ground inside this earthen parapet is the remains of an old ammunition pit or powder magazine. Usually a roof of heavy timbers and six to ten inches of packed dirt covered the ammunition and powder stored here. More powder magazines are visible along the trail as you continue up to the summit of Maryland Heights.

8. Cliffs. These precipitous cliffs are comprised of *Harpers shale*, a dark blue-gray rock made up of intensely metamorphosed shales and sandstones (see **Appalachian Geology**, page 81). The Potomac and Shenandoah rivers converge just below.

Retrace the orange-blazed trail back up the mountain.

9. Six-Gun Battery. This fortification, also known as the 30-Pounder Battery, was built in October 1862. Six 30-pounder Parrott rifles and two 24-pounder siege guns here commanded Loudoun and Bolivar Heights, protecting Harpers Ferry against assault from either quarter. A powder magazine is visible just inside this parapet.

Turn right in front of the Six-Gun Battery to continue on the orange-blazed trail. This trail crosses some rough ground and is hard to follow in places. You may also proceed straight through the Six-Gun Battery on an unmarked trail which eventually rejoins the orange-blazed trail further up the mountain.

10. 100-Pounder Battery. A massive 100-pounder Parrott rifle weighing nearly five tons—the heaviest and longest range cannon on Maryland Heights—formerly stood here. This potent weapon could fire a projectile weighing anywhere from 70 to 100 pounds. More powder magazines can be found in this area.

11. Maryland Heights Summit. The summit here, marked by a small survey disc, is 1,448 feet above sea level—the highest point in the Harpers Ferry area.

12. Stone Fort. Union engineers, using contraband slaves living behind Federal lines as the principal source of labor, began erecting this fort in October 1862. A larger Main Fort, containing embrasures for artillery along its north wall, was built around the Stone Fort. These embrasures

Jubal Early's Raid on Washington

In July 1864, Lt. Col. Jubal A. Early commanded Second Corps of the Army of Northern Virginia, a force comprised of 12,000 Confederate infantry and some 2,000 cavalry. With this modest contingent, Early intended to strike at Washington, D.C., from the Shenandoah Valley and divert as many Union forces as possible from the siege of Petersburg, Virginia.

On July 4, Early advanced against Harpers Ferry. The Union garrison withdrew across the Potomac River to Maryland Heights while Federal engineers destroyed the B&O Railroad bridge behind them. Early's Second Corps, unable to cross the Potomac River here and under fire from Federal gunners on Maryland Heights, marched northwest to Shepherdstown and crossed the Potomac at Packhorse (Blackford's) Ford.

The Union force on Maryland Heights was comprised of six regiments of infantry, about 1,000 effective cavalry, another 2,500 dismounted cavalry, and about 40 cannon, all under the command of Maj. Gen. Franz Sigel. Early approached the Union stronghold from the west, but found it too well fortified to carry by assault. Skirting to the north, the Confederate army instead advanced to Frederick, Maryland, where on July 9 they easily routed Union Gen. Lew Wallace in the Battle of the Monocacy.

On July 12, Early's Second Corps marched down the Seventh Street Pike to the northern outskirts of Washington. Confronted once again by strong Union fortifications at Fort Stevens, the Confederates withdrew and retreated back into Virginia. Early's daring thrust at Washington neither seriously threatened the nation's capital nor caused Union commanders to interrupt their seige of Petersburg.

held seven light guns—mostly howitzers—and one 30-pounder Parrott. This arrangement was designed to prevent Confederate forces from attacking the heights from the north, as they had successfully done under General Lafayette McLaws just one month earlier.

13. Military Camp. Although completely overgrown today, this area once served as home for the thousand-man Union garrison that defended Maryland Heights. The scattered ruins of stone tent bases, chimneys, and ovens are barely visible today.

Continue down the mountain on the old military road to your starting point.

Loudoun Heights

Allow about three hours for this walking tour. Start at the small dirt parking lot on Shenandoah Street just off U.S. Route 340. Walk across the Shenandoah River bridge and turn right over the guard rail onto the white-blazed trail. Begin a fairly steep climb up to the crest of Loudoun Heights.

1. Appalachian Trail. The Appalachian Trail was relocated to this spot in late 1985 after a new footbridge was opened across the Potomac River in the Lower Town of Harpers Ferry. Formerly the trail followed the crest of Loudoun Heights farther north and crossed the Potomac River on the U.S. Route 340 bridge, bypassing Harpers Ferry. From 1936-1949, before either of the present U.S. 340 bridges were built, hikers crossed over to Harpers Ferry from the base of Loudoun Heights on a rope-drawn ferry and then crossed the Potomac River on the Bollman highway bridge.

Today, the Appalachian Trail is the longest marked footpath in the world, stretching over 2,000 miles from Maine to Georgia.

2. Military Road. The abandoned road that parallels the trail here was probably constructed by the government sometime after 1827 to provide access to Armory timberland on Loudoun Heights. During the first year of the Civil War, this road was used by the Confederate army to move

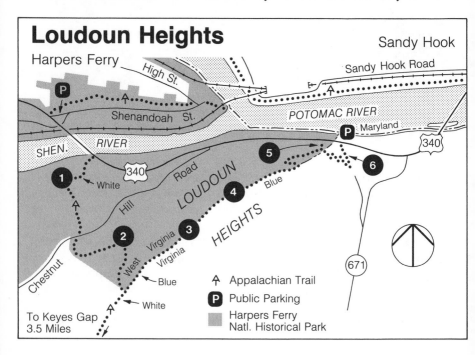

troops and supplies to the summit of the mountain. In September-October 1862, the road was rebuilt by the Second Division of Twelfth Corps, Army of the Potomac, who were encamped on Loudoun Heights.

Turn left at the crest of the mountain and continue on the blue-blazed trail.

3. Armory Timberland. In 1813, the U.S. Government leased 1,395 acres of woodland on Loudoun Heights, "For the purchase of the trees, timber and woods." Along the ridgetop here colliers stayed beside smoking charcoal mounds, tending to the ten-day process by which timber was converted into charcoal. The charcoal in turn was used to fuel the furnaces and forges of the U.S. Armory in Harpers Ferry.

Upland Hardwood Forest

The river slopes and ridgetops in the Harpers Ferry area are comprised of an oak-hickory forest. White oak, named for its pale gray bark, is a common tree here. Its wood is the sturdiest of all the oaks. Chestnut oak has a system of branching roots which enables it to grow on the rocky mountainsides. Hickory wood is extremely resilient, making it ideal for the handles of axes and sledges. Red oak and black oak are also common to this woodland, and together with all these trees make up the forest canopy or overstory.

The understory of the oak-hickory forest is comprised of young oaks and hickories and a variety of smaller trees. Sassafras produces a flavorful pink tea which is extracted from its root bark. Dogwood blossoms with soft white flowers in May and turns to a vivid scarlet in October. Eastern redbud blossoms with pinkish to lavender flowers and has a scaly, reddish-brown bark. The red-eyes vireo, a small bird with a prominent black-bordered white stripe over its eyes, lives in this understory.

A shrub layer below the understory consists of woody-stemmed plants three to 12 feet tall. Virginia creeper and sumac are common here and generally herald the coming of fall by turning bright red. Catbirds and woodthrushes frequent these shrubs.

A herb layer features ferns, grasses, mosses, and other shade-tolerant plants. Jewelweed, or touch-me-not, blooms here in July with small orange cup-like flowers. Juice from its stems is a good treatment for poison ivy, and the two often grow together. Toads, sparrows, and chipmunks commonly feed in this layer.

On the forest floor mushrooms and other fungi decompose dead organic matter, recycling vital minerals to the soil for use by the living plant and animal community.

The confluence of the Potomac and Shenandoah rivers from Loudoun Heights.

By the 1850s, the wood supply on the north slope and crest of Loudoun Heights had been nearly exhausted. The situation was exacerbated by a forest fire in April 1851. Major John Symington, Superintendent of the Armory, wrote that "a fire was observed on the Government land, some distance up the north face of the Mountain oppisite [sic] to the Rifle Factory, which urged by a strong North West wind soon begain [sic] to spread rapidly.... The ground burnt over may be estimated at 200 acres, the greater part of which was a body of thrifty young timber of some twelve or fifteen years growth."

4. Infantry Fortifications. After the Confederate troops of Brig. Gen. John G. Walker occupied Loudoun Heights without opposition on September 14, 1862, Union engineers constructed infantry trenches and stone fortifications along the crest of this ridge (see **Stonewall Jackson Captures Harpers Ferry,** page 74). Between September-December 1862, soldiers of the Second Division of Twelfth Corps, Army of the Potomac, erected about 35 stone redoubts and rifle pits. A signal station was also built.

5. Cliffs. The rocks that comprise these cliffs and the ledges which cross the Potomac River directly below are *Weverton quartzite,* a whitish rock with milky quartz grains. Intense heat and pressure, exerted when shifts in the earth's crust raised up the Appalachian Mountains, created this hard metamorphic rock out of sedimentary rock.

You can return the way you came or descend the mountain from here on a series of steep switchbacks. Watch for traffic when you reach U.S. Route 340.

Appalachian Geology

At the dawn of the Paleozoic Era, 600 million years ago, a great depression in the earth's crust—the Appalachian geosyncline—extended from Alabama to Newfoundland. A broad, shallow sea spread across this trough. Here erosional debris from ancient land masses slowly gathered. Sediments accumulated in layers to a depth of several thousand feet, becoming compacted and cemented into sedimentary rocks. Sand particles became sandstone, clay and silt combined to form shale, and the decaying remains of plants and animals—corals, sponges, trilobites, brachiopods—were lithified into limestone.

Toward the close of the Paleozoic Era, about 230 million years ago, tremendous pressure exerted from the southeast drove the earth's crust westward, compressing the strata of the Appalachian geosyncline into parallel faults and folds. Along the eastern edge of the geosyncline, in an area extending north-south from Pennsylvania to Virginia, this "Appalachian Revolution" forced up an immense fold in the earth's crust called the South Mountain anticlinorium. South Mountain, Short Hill Mountain, Maryland Heights, Loudoun Heights, and Bolivar Heights are all second-order folds within this massive formation.

The tremendous forces that created the South Mountain anticlinorium also subjected the rock strata to intense heat and pressure. Sedimentary rocks were metamorphosed, their internal structure being altered or altogether changed. In the Harpers Ferry area, sandstone became quartzite (*Weverton quartzite*) and shale became a schist, slate or phyllite (*Harpers shale*).

6. Harpers Ferry & Hillsborough Turnpike. The trail here travels briefly along the old route of the Harpers Ferry & Hillsborough Turnpike (now Virginia Route 671). In May 1851, the newly formed Harpers Ferry & Hillsborough Turnpike Company asked the federal government for permission to construct a turnpike through Armory timberland along the base of Loudoun Heights. A right-of-way was granted, and a stone Dwelling House on the south side of the Shenandoah River was also leased to the company for use as a toll house. In return, the turnpike company agreed to provide toll-free passage to Armory workmen traveling to and from the government's Loudoun Heights timberland.

Virginia Route 671 was re-routed away from the old road you now stand on when the present U.S. Route 340 bridges across the Potomac and Shenandoah rivers were completed in 1949.

Bolivar Heights

Allow about a half hour for this walking tour.

1. Bolivar, West Virginia. On December 29, 1825, Bolivar (pronounced like "Oliver") was given town status by the Virginia Assembly. It was during this same year that the South American patriot Simon Bolivar, for whom this town is named, realized independence for his own country. Previously known as "Mudfort," the Bolivar of 1825 was a village of just 270 people.

2. Infantry Trenches. Bolivar Heights saw considerable action during the Civil War. On October 16, 1861, a sharp skirmish was fought here between Col. Turner Ashby's Virginia militia and Union regulars under the command of Col. John W. Geary. The Battle of Bolivar Heights, as this fracas became known, was inconclusive for either side.

On May 30, 1862, Maj. Gen. Thomas "Stonewall" Jackson's Valley Army energetically demonstrated against Union forces entrenched on

Stonewall Jackson's Valley Campaign

In late April 1862, one of the Civil War's most celebrated military campaigns began. Maj. Gen. Thomas "Stonewall" Jackson and his 9,500-man Valley Army were holed up at Swift Run Gap in the Blue Ridge. The Confederates had been chased there by Maj. Gen. Nathaniel P. Banks, who commanded 22,000 Union troops at nearby Harrisonburg.

In the weeks that followed, Jackson maneuvered his army around the Shenandoah Valley swiftly and relentlessly, engaging Union forces at McDowell, Front Royal, Winchester, and Harpers Ferry. Banks, joined in the Valley by the armies of Brig. Gen. James Shields and Maj. Gen. John C. Fremont, desperately tried to catch Jackson and inflict a mortal blow to his Valley Army. But the Union generals engaged Jackson piecemeal, unable to bring their substantial manpower advantage to bear. By June 12, 1862, both Fremont and Shields were retreating back into the northern Shenandoah Valley, having suffered decisive defeats at Port Republic and Cross Keyes, respectively.

During the six weeks following April 30, 1862, the Valley Army had marched almost 400 miles. They defeated Union forces in five separate battles and engaged in almost daily skirmishing. On June 18, Jackson led his men across the Blue Ridge and east to Richmond, where they joined in the Seven Days battles.

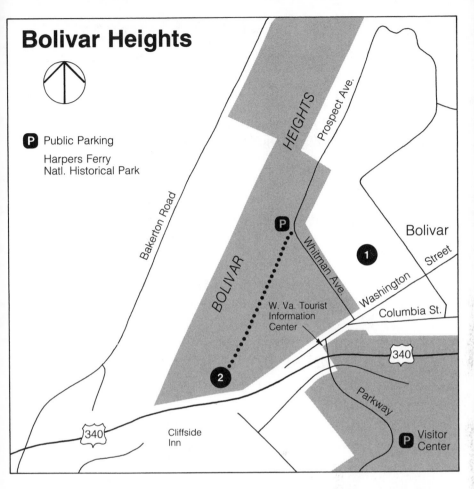

Bolivar Heights

Harpers Ferry
Natl. Historical Park

P Public Parking

HEIGHTS
Prospect Ave.
Bakerton Road
BOLIVAR
Whitman Ave.
Bolivar
Washington
Street
Columbia St.
W. Va. Tourist
Information
Center
340
Parkway
340
Cliffside
Inn
Visitor
Center

Bolivar Heights, probing for weak points along the Federal front. But when three separate Union armies threatened the Shenandoah Valley at Front Royal, Martinsburg, and Strasburg, Jackson withdrew.

The most noteworthy action here took place on September 13-15, 1862. On the 13th Jackson, advancing to School House Ridge just beyond Bolivar Heights, sealed a trap that snared the 12,500-man Union garrison at Harpers Ferry (see **Stonewall Jackson Captures Harpers Ferry**, page 74). Cannon fire from Loudoun and Maryland Heights, also in Confederate hands, left the Union forces in desperate straights. On the morning of September 15, the Union commanders held a council of war on Bolivar Heights. Surrounded by a force double the size of their own and out of long range artillery ammunition, the officers unanimously agreed to surrender. At around 9:00 am, white flags were raised by Union troops all along this ridge.

C&O Canal–Fort Duncan

Allow about two and a half hours for this complete walking tour.

1. Harpers Ferry Road. On the evening of October 16, 1859—shortly before 10:30 pm—John Brown, the fanatical abolitionist, traveled down the hill here with 18 other men. The group had set out from the Kennedy Farm, their secret hideaway, just a few miles up the road. The men walked silently, concealing Sharps rifles under long gray overcoats. With them was a horse-drawn wagon carrying a sledge hammer, crowbar, and several pikes.

These men were bound for Harpers Ferry, and were intent on seizing the U.S. Armory and Arsenal. The guns they found there, according to John Brown's plan, would arm a rebellion of slaves (see **John Brown's Raid**, page 28).

2. Lock 34. Also known as Goodheart's Lock. The dimensions of lift locks along the Chesapeake & Ohio Canal were standardized at 15 feet wide by 98 feet long. This permitted barges measuring 14 1/2 feet by 92 feet to

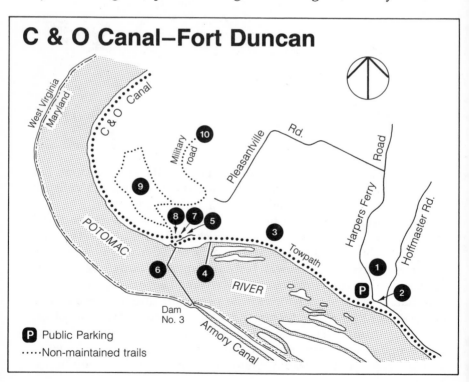

C & O Canal–Fort Duncan

P Public Parking
····· Non-maintained trails

Canal boat passing through Inlet Lock No. 3. The old mule crossover bridge is in the background. (National Park Service photo).

snugly pass through. A brick lockhouse which formerly stood on the river side of this lock was washed away by the Flood of 1936. See also **Chesapeake & Ohio Canal**, page 73.

3. Harpers Shale. The angular cliffs on the far ("berm") side of the canal here are comprised of *Harpers shale*. This dark blue-gray rock, which consists of intensely metamorphosed shales and sandstones, extends north-south in a belt about 2,000 feet thick. The tremendous fold was created some 230 million years ago when shifts in the earth's crust formed the Appalachian Mountains (see **Appalachian Geology**, page 81).

This belt of *Harpers shale* also makes up "The Needles" rapids on the adjacent Potomac River and "The Staircase" rapids on the nearby Shenandoah River.

4. Unfinished Armory Dam. In February 1859, the U.S. Government let a contract for the construction of a new dam across the Potomac River. This structure was intended to replace the old U.S. Potomac Dam (Dam No. 3) as the source of waterpower for the Musket Factory in Harpers Ferry. Snovell & Company, the appointed contractor, began laying masonry for the new dam on the Maryland side of the river in June 1859. Plans called for the dam to be built of stone and to have a timber superstructure.

The contractor, however, made such slow progress that in October 1859, the U.S. Government cancelled its contract. Of a proposed length of 1,470 feet, Snovell & Company had succeeded in erecting only 335 feet. A second contractor fared little better, lengthening the dam to just 420 feet by November 1860.

Construction was interrupted by the Civil War, and this dam was never completed.

5. Mule Crossover Bridge. The original towpath crossed the feeder intake canal here across to Lock 35 on a wooden mule crossover bridge.

6. Dam No. 3. On August 9, 1799, the U.S. Government began erecting the Armory Dam or U.S. Potomac Dam. Completed a year later, this dam furnished power to turn the water wheels and turbines of the Musket Factory for the next 60 years. But with periodic flooding and with the ever increasing power demands of new gun-making machinery, the government was forced to repair or rebuild this dam on several occasions.

In 1832-1833, this dam also began serving the C&O Canal—this being the third of seven dams along the Potomac River used to supply water to the canal. Water was admitted into the canal here through Inlet Lock No. 3. This lock also permitted barges carrying coal and other supplies bound for the Musket Factory to cross the Potomac River and proceed down the Armory Canal on the far side of the river.

7. Lock 36. The C&O Canal numbered their locks consecutively, beginning with Lock 1 in Georgetown and ending with Lock 75 at North Branch near Cumberland. But in fact, the canal had only 74 lift locks. As a cost-saving measure, engineers built only three locks at Paw Paw Tunnel where four were originally planned, enlarging the lift of each of these locks from eight to about 10 feet.

8. Lock 35. The drydock on the far side of this lock was used sporadically in the 1800s. Here barges could be set out of water and leaks repaired with tin and tar.

The old military road up to Fort Duncan is not maintained and is difficult to follow in late spring, summer, and early fall.

9. Iron Ore Quarry. In these woods, along a fault line separating *Harpers shale* from a series of limestones, Cambro-Ordovician limonite ores of the finest quality were quarried during much of the 1800s. This deposit was commonly known as the "Maryland bank." Ore quarried here was shipped primarily to Antietam Ironworks about seven miles upstream for processing into pig iron.

10. Fort Duncan. This earthen fort was built during the Civil War as part of the Union defensive network around Harpers Ferry. In 1864, Fort Duncan consisted of a 15-foot earthen wall surrounded by a wide, dry ditch. Sixteen guns were positioned here, and there were three magazines.

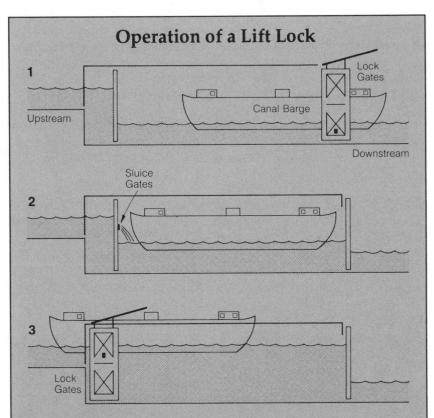

Operation of a Lift Lock

1. A canal barge, headed upstream, enters the lock. The upstream gates, which are closed, hold back the water of the next "level."

2. Once within the lock, the downstream lock gates are shut. Small sluice gates on the upstream lock gates are opened, admitting water into the lock chamber. As the lock chamber is filled, the canal barge is slowly raised.

3. When the lock chamber is filled to the height of the upstream water level. the upstream lock gates are opened and the canal boat proceeds. This procedure is reversed for boats headed downstream. It generally took a canal barge from 10 to 15 minutes to pass through a lock in this manner.

Weverton–South Mountain

Allow about two and a half hours for this walking tour. To reach the stone headgate ruins on the Potomac River, you must bushwack across muddy streambeds and through thick underbrush.

1. Stone Headgates. A 15-foot-high dam, erected sometime before 1846, diverted water from the Potomac River into these three large stone intake sluices. This water was then channeled down a long headrace where building sites for water-powered mills were offered for lease. During periods of high water, however, this headrace caused problems for the adjacent C&O Canal. After the Flood of 1877, the canal company purchased this property and demolished the dam. The ruins of the "Loughridge Mill for sawing Stone"—one of the few mills to actually be built here—stand at the downstream end of these stone headgates. See **Weverton, 1849** map, page 93.

2. Lock 31. This lift lock was completed in 1833. The two piles of stone blocks adjacent to the towpath here originally formed the lock's towpath wall. When this wall began to settle and to gradually tilt inward, these blocks were removed and replaced with the concrete you see today. The opposite lock wall still consists of the original stone blocks.

The B&O Railroad and C&O Canal, bitter rivals for many years, traveled side by side just upstream from Weverton. (National Park Service photo).

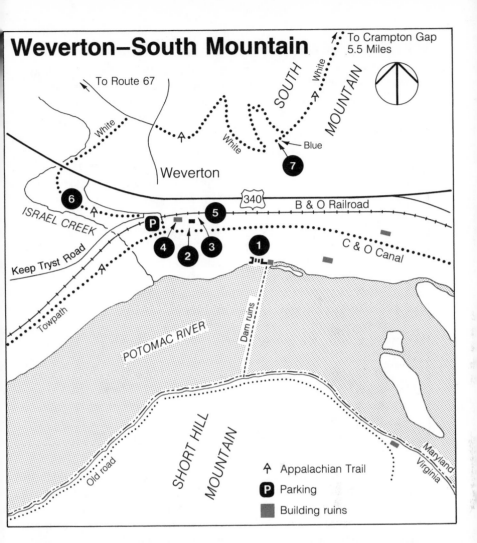

Weverton–South Mountain

To Crampton Gap
5.5 Miles

To Route 67

SOUTH MOUNTAIN

White

White

Blue

7

White

Weverton

340

B & O Railroad

6

ISRAEL CREEK

P

5

4

2

3

1

C & O Canal

Keep Tryst Road

Towpath

POTOMAC RIVER

Dam ruins

Maryland
Virginia

SHORT HILL MOUNTAIN

Old road

⚡ Appalachian Trail

P Parking

Building ruins

3. Harpers Ferry & Frederick Turnpike. This old road is recognizable today only as a shallow depression in the ground between the lockhouse and railroad tracks. Built in 1832, the turnpike ran from Frederick to the Maryland abutment of Wager's Bridge at Harpers Ferry. C&O Canal Company records indicate that many travelers tried to avoid paying a turnpike toll by instead using the towpath to reach Harpers Ferry from here.

4. Weverton Grist Mill. The original mill, erected in 1774, was torn down and replaced with a three-story frame mill in 1856. A long headrace supplied water from Israel Creek, turning the mill's water

Baltimore & Ohio Railroad

On July 4, 1828, construction was begun on the Baltimore & Ohio Railroad—the very same day that construction commenced on the Chesapeake & Ohio Canal. Both railroad and canal proved to be bitter rivals until the B&O became the canal's major bond-holder after the Flood of 1889.

At Point of Rocks, about eight miles downstream from here, the two companies engaged in their first dispute. Here the B&O secured an injunction against canal construction, contesting the right-of-way along a narrow shelf of land bordered by high cliffs and the Potomac River. In 1832, the courts ruled in the canal's favor. But lacking much-needed capital, the canal company made an agreement with the railroad whereby the B&O was allowed to proceed west to Harpers Ferry alongside the canal. The B&O, in turn, would subscribe to 2,500 shares of canal stock. It was further agreed that a tight board fence be erected between the railroad and canal to keep train engines from frightening canal mules. But rather than carry out this provision, the B&O compromised by limiting operation to horse power between Point of Rocks and Harpers Ferry until 1836.

In December 1834, the B&O reached the Maryland shore opposite Harpers Ferry. In November 1842, the railroad was opened to Cumberland, Maryland—eight years before the canal was completed.

wheel and driving four pair of burr-stones. A stone intake arch which still stands admitted additional water from the canal when Israel Creek was running low. The mill owners purchased this supplementary water under the terms of a lease granted by the C&O Canal Company. Wastewater leaving the mill's water wheel passed under Lock 31 through a tailrace culvert which is still intact.

5. Baltimore & Ohio Railroad. The original line of the B&O Railroad was completed here in 1834. A recent decision by the present owners of the railroad—CSX Corporation—has done away with the B&O name.

6. Appalachian Trail. This 2,000-mile-long recreational footpath, which was initially completed in 1937, today extends from Maine to Georgia. The trail traverses 14 states, two national parks, and eight national forests.

Ruins of "A large stone Flour Mill" at the foot of Short Hill Mountain across the Potomac River from Weverton.

Casper Wever

In 1834, Casper Wever, a former chief engineer of the Baltimore & Ohio Railroad, purchased 500 acres at the foot of Pleasant Valley and the flowage rights on both sides of the Potomac River from Harpers Ferry to the foot of South Mountain. The Weverton Manufacturing Company was chartered by the Maryland General Assembly and Wever began to erect a dam across the Potomac River.

Wever's dam diverted water into headraces on both sides of the Potomac River. Along these headraces Wever offered leases to waterpowered factories and to parcels of land, attempting to attract industry onto his property.

In 1846, the Henderson Steel & File Manufacturing Company located at Weverton and operated a factory here until the Civil War. Also in about 1846, William Loughridge began to operate a small marble works in a building adjacent to Wever's dam and stone headgates. Across the river in Virginia, "A large stone Flour Mill" was erected.

Excessive lease rates, however, discouraged other companies from locating at Weverton, and Wever's dream of establishing a sizeable industrial community here was never realized. Wever died in 1849, leaving behind little more than a small village that still bears his name.

Shortly after Wever's death, the Potomac Company purchased 300 feet of river frontage, built a new dam across the Potomac, and erected a large cotton factory. Unfortunately, the affairs of the company became seriously entangled and this mill never operated. After the Flood of 1877, the C&O Canal Company purchased the Potomac Company's dam and cotton factory. The dam was promptly demolished and in 1879, the cotton mill was torn down.

After passing through the small village of Weverton, the trail begins a steady climb up South Mountain.

7. Weverton Cliffs. South Mountain is an anticline—an arch of stratified rock in which the layers are bent downward from the crest. This immense fold was created some 230 million years ago when the Appalachian Mountains were first raised up (see **Appalachian Geology**, page 81).

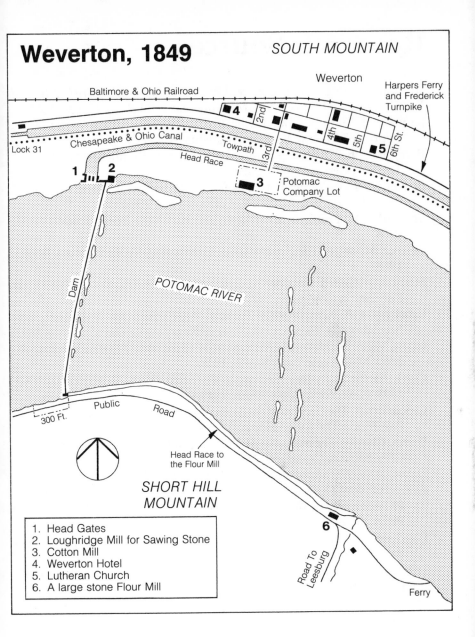

Weverton, 1849

SOUTH MOUNTAIN

Weverton

Harpers Ferry
and Frederick
Turnpike

Baltimore & Ohio Railroad

4 2nd

Chesapeake & Ohio Canal

Lock 31

Towpath

3rd

Head Race

4th
5th
5
6th St.

1 **2**

3 Potomac
Company Lot

Dam

POTOMAC RIVER

300 Ft.

Public   Road

Head Race to
the Flour Mill

SHORT HILL
MOUNTAIN

6

Road To Leesburg

Ferry

1. Head Gates
2. Loughridge Mill for Sawing Stone
3. Cotton Mill
4. Weverton Hotel
5. Lutheran Church
6. A large stone Flour Mill

93

Research Sources

Anthony, Kate J., *Storer College, Harpers Ferry, W. Va., Brief Historical Sketch, 1867-1891.* Boston: Morning Star Publishing House, 1891.

Bagnall, William R., *The Textile Industries of the United States.* 1893. Reprinted in New York by Augustus M. Kelley, 1971.

Barry, Joseph, *The Strange Story of Harper's Ferry.* Shepherdstown, W.Va.: The Shepherdstown Register, 1903.

Becker, Carl M., "James Leffel: Double Turbine Water Wheel Inventor," *Ohio History,* Vol. 75, No. 4, Autumn 1966, 200-211.

Brockman, C. Frank, *Trees of North America.* New York: Golden Press, 1968.

Brooks, Maurice, *The Appalachians.* Grantsville, W.Va.: Seneca Books, 1968.

Bushong, Millard Kessler, *Historic Jefferson County.* Boyce, Va.: Carr Publishing Company, 1972.

Catalogue of the New American Turbine, Manufactured by The Dayton Globe Iron Works Co., Successors to Stout, Mills & Temple. Dayton, Ohio, 1892.

Clark, Victor S., *History of Manufactures in the United States, Vol. 1, 1607-1860.* New York: Peter Smith, 1949.

Clark, Victor S., *History of Manufactures in the United States, Vol. 2, 1860-1893.* New York: Peter Smith, 1949.

Cloos, Ernst, *The Geology of the South Mountain Anticlinorium, Maryland.* Baltimore: The Johns Hopkins Press, 1950.

Davis, Charles Thomas, *The Manufacture of Paper.* Philadelphia: Henry Clay Baird & Company, 1886.

Davis, Julia, *The Shenandoah.* New York: Farrar & Rinehart, 1945.

Evans, Oliver, *The Young Mill-wright and Miller's Guide,* 13th Edition. Philadelphia: Lea & Blanchard, 1850. Reprinted in New York by Arno Press, 1972.

Everhart, William C., *A History of Harpers Ferry.* Harpers Ferry: National Park Service, 1952.

Freeman, Douglas Southall, *George Washington, Vol. 1.* New York: Charles Scribner's Sons, 1948.

Freeman, Douglas Southall, *George Washington, Vol. 6.* New York, Charles Scribner's Sons, 1954.

Guthiem, Frederick, *The Potomac.* New York: Grosset & Dunlop, 1968.

Hahn, Thomas F., *George Washington's Canal at Great Falls, Virginia.* Shepherdstown, W.Va.: American Canal & Transportation Center, 1976.

Hahn, Thomas F., *Towpath Guide to the C&O Canal.* Shepherdstown, W.Va.: American Canal & Transportation Center, 1982.

Hannah, David, *Archeological Excavations on Virginius Island, 1966-68.* Harpers Ferry: Jobs Corp Civilian Conservation Center, 1969.

Hindle, Brooke, editor, *America's Wooden Age: Aspects of its Early Technology.* Tarrytown, N.Y.: Sleepy Hollow Restorations, 1976.

Hungerford, Edward, *The Story of the Baltimore & Ohio Railroad, 1827-1927.* Vols. 1-2. New York: G.P. Putnam's Sons, 1928.

John Brown's Raid. Washington, D.C.: National Park Service, 1973.

Kytle, Elizabeth, *Home on the Canal.* Cabin John, Md.: Seven Locks Press, 1983.

Land Records of Jefferson County, Virginia.

McGrain, John W., "Mills of Washington County, Maryland." 1967.

Mead, Daniel W., *Water Power Engineering.* New York: McGraw-Hill Book Company, 1915.

Mongin, Alfred, *Research Report, A College In Secessia, The Early Years of Storer College.* Harpers Ferry: Harpers Ferry National Monument, 1960.

Murfin, James V., *The Gleam of Bayonets.* New York: Bonanza Books, 1965.

Quarles, Benjamin, *Allies For Freedom, Blacks and John Brown.* New York: Oxford University Press, 1974.

Reports on the Water-Power of the United States, Census Office, Department of the Interior, Part 1. Washington, D.C.: Government Printing Office, 1885.

Rothfuss, Joel F., *Geological History of the Harpers Ferry Area.* Harpers Ferry: National Park Service, 1970.

Sanderlin, Walter S., *The Great National Project, A History of the Chesapeake & Ohio Canal.* Baltimore: The Johns Hopkins Press, 1946.

Sarles, Frank B., Jr., *Economic and Social History of Virginius Island.* Washington, D.C.: National Park Service, 1969.

Savery Papers. Harpers Ferry National Historical Park.

Smith, Merrit Roe, *Harpers Ferry Armory and the New Technology.* Ithaca, N.Y.: Cornell University Press, 1977.

Smith, Philip R., Jr., *History of Loudoun Heights, 1813-1880.* Harpers Ferry: National Park Service, 1959.

Snell, Charles W., *A Compendium of the Commercial and Industrial Advertisements of the Business and Manufacturing Establishments of Harpers Ferry and the Island of Virginius, 1824-1861, Virginia.* Denver: National Park Service, 1973.

Snell, Charles W., *A Short History of the Island of Virginius, 1816-1870.* Harpers Ferry: National Park Service, 1959.

Snell, Charles W., *Historical Data, Historic Structure Report, The Nichols/Williams Building.* Denver: National Park Service, 1980.

Snell, Charles W., *Historic Structures (Ruins) Report, Part 1, for The Large and Small Arsenal Buildings.* Harpers Ferry: National Park Service, 1959.

Snell, Charles W., *The Business Enterprises and Commercial Development of Harpers Ferry's Lower Town Area, 1803 to 1861*. Harpers Ferry: National Park Service, 1973.

Snell, Charles W., *The Town of Harpers Ferry in 1859, a Physical History*. Harpers Ferry: National Park Service, 1959.

Snell, Charles W., and Philip R. Smith, Jr., *The Musket Factory Buildings and Grounds, Harpers Ferry Armory, 1859-1860*. Harpers Ferry: National Park Service, 1959.

Stinson, Dwight E., *The First Railroad Bridge at Harpers Ferry*. Harpers Ferry: National Park Service, 1970.

Sullivan, Arthur L., *Harpers Ferry in the Civil War, 1862*. Harpers Ferry: National Park Service, 1961.

Thompson, Michael D., *The Iron Industry in Western Maryland*. 1976.

Toogood, Anna Coxe, *The Lockwood House, Birthplace of Storer College*. National Park Service, Division of History, Office of Archeology and Historic Preservation, January 3, 1969.